D0908162

READING THE RUSSIAN LANGUAGE

BOOKS IN
LIBRARY AND INFORMATION SCIENCE

A Series of Monographs and Textbooks

EDITOR
ALLEN KENT

Director, Office of Communications Programs
University of Pittsburgh
Pittsburgh, Pennsylvania

Volume 1. CLASSIFIED LIBRARY OF CONGRESS SUBJECT HEADINGS, Volume 1—CLASSIFIED LIST, edited by James G. Williams, Martha L. Manheimer, and Jay E. Daily.

Volume 2. CLASSIFIED LIBRARY OF CONGRESS SUBJECT HEADINGS, Volume 2 — ALPHABETIC LIST, edited by James G. Williams, Martha L. Manheimer, and Jay E. Daily.

Volume 3. ORGANIZING NONPRINT MATERIALS by Jay E. Daily.

Volume 4. COMPUTER-BASED CHEMICAL INFORMATION, edited by Edward McC. Arnett and Allen Kent.

Volume 5. STYLE MANUAL: A GUIDE FOR THE PREPARATION OF REPORTS AND DISSERTATIONS by Martha L. Manheimer.

Volume 6. THE ANATOMY OF CENSORSHIP by Jay E. Daily.

Volume 8. RESOURCE SHARING IN LIBRARIES: WHY • HOW • WHEN • NEXT ACTION STEPS, edited by Allen Kent.

Volume 9. READING THE RUSSIAN LANGUAGE: A GUIDE FOR LIBRARIANS AND OTHER PROFESSIONALS by Rosalind Kent.

Volumes in Preparation

Volume 7. INFORMATION SCIENCE: SEARCH FOR IDENTITY, edited by Anthony Debons.

Volume 10. DOCUMENT RETRIEVAL SYSTEMS: FACTORS AFFECTING SEARCH TIME by K. Leon Montgomery.
CATALOGING AND CLASSIFICATION: A WORKBOOK by Martha L. Manheimer.

Additional volumes in preparation

Reading the Russian Language
a guide for librarians
and other professionals

Rosalind Kent

MARCEL DEKKER, INC., New York   1974

MARCEL DEKKER, INC.
305 East 45th Street, New York, New York 10017

LIBRARY OF CONGRESS CATALOG CARD NUMBER 74-81799

ISBN 0-8247-6236-3

PRINTED IN THE UNITED STATES OF AMERICA

PREFACE

Some 15 years ago, I found myself looking forward to a trip to the Soviet Union
accompanying my husband for business purposes.
It seemed logical to try to learn something
of the language and I began to do so at an
Adult Education class in our local High School.
This led to an arrangement with the instructor for private tutoring. After a year of
intensive study I began to translate technical
material under the critical eyes of a kindly
editor (or should I say the kindly eyes of a
critical editor).

When I had gained more confidence, I
undertook the translation of L. I. Guten-
makher's *Electronic Information-Logic Machines*
(New York, 1963) for John Wiley & Sons.

I was also translating and abstracting
Russian material for a number of industrial
and governmental organizations.

In 1965, a new course was introduced in
the School of Library and Information Sciences
at the University of Pittsburgh - Russian
for Librarians. The instructor contracted
to teach the course was unable to do so and
I undertook to develop and teach it. I did
so for five years.

This effort is the result of a desire
to produce a text for self study and for the
aid of instructors who may not wish to use
the traditional teaching methods and can

benefit from someone who learned the hard
way.

I want to express my heartfelt thanks
and appreciation to my very devoted husband
Allen who patiently edited many of my translations and my book through the years and
who urged and encouraged me to write this
text. Also to my children Merryl, Emily,
Jacqueline and Carolyn who had to bear with
Mom and "her Russian" in their growing years.

Rosalind Kent

Mt. Lebanon, Pennsylvania

TABLE OF CONTENTS

CONTENTS vii

INTRODUCTION

The objective of this book is to teach Russian to librarians who have never tried to learn the language or who have tried and given up. The objective is a limited one - it is to teach only to read specialized material which would be of use to the librarian. What will this accomplish? It will permit the librarian to select and acquire materials and to perform minimal reference service.

My philosophy of instruction in designing the text is to motivate the student early in the game by making it possible for him to use the language for productive purposes (with some trepidation, of course) even after the first chapter.

The key to making this happen is the ability to use a Russian-English dictionary; but this is not possible without first having a knowledge of the Russian alphabet.

Therefore, Chapter I begins with an introduction to the Russian alphabet and its English transliteration. Knowing the sounds of the Russian letters permits the librarian to pronounce words. This makes it possible to search the dictionary more efficiently without returning to each letter in the word. It also enables the librarian to identify cognates.

The dictionary which I have found most useful in preparing this text and to which

I refer consistently is B. A. Lapidus and
S. V. Shevtsova's *The Learner's Russian-English Dictionary* (Cambridge, The M.I.T. Press,
1963). I consider this particular dictionary
helpful to students because unlike most other
Russian-English dictionaries, in addition to
definitions it identifies the genders, parts
of speech and endings for many words - so
vital to translating the Russian language.

I have introduced in the chapters following, many principles of Russian grammar,
citing examples of usage in each case to
clarify the explanations. Only those gram-
matical principles were selected which I felt
were most important in this short course of
14 chapters. By drawing from my experience
in teaching the course to raw beginners, I
have found that these principles provided a
good basis for covering the needs of the
librarian.

Following the explanations in each chapter, is a translation exercise which makes
use of the newly learned principle. On the
pages following, the exercise is translated
and a full explanation is provided with definitions derived from the Lapidus-Shevtsova
dictionary. At the conclusion of the chapter
an excerpt from a Russian reading is presented
for independent work. It should be within
the capability of the student to complete this
exercise utilizing his knowledge of the material presented in the preceding chapters.
For this reason it would be wise to preserve
the sequence of the textbook when using it
for independent study.

Throughout the text, terminology has
been used to further familiarize the student
with the langauge as it appears in the field

of librarianship. At the end of each chapter
the new terminology introduced in the chapter
is reproduced with definitions. In the back
of the book, an alphabetical compilation of
all these terms*is listed for easy reference.

It should be noted that the definitions
appear in the footnotes in two forms. The
lengthy form is derived from the dictionary.
The shorter one is from the listing referred
to above.

For those who are interested in using
this text for independent study, the best
approach would be the following:

1. Learn the alphabet

2. Translate the practise exercises
after the presentation of each new principle.
If more detailed explanations are required,
I have found M. H. Fayer, A. Pressman, A. F.
Pressman *Simplified Russian Grammar* (New York,
1957) most helpful.

3. Compare your translation with the one
provided for the practise exercise.

4. Try the concluding exercise for further practise.

5. Memorize new words and definitions
given at the end of each chapter.

As soon as possible try to reinforce
your knowledge of the language by translating
book titles, title pages and tables of contents. By the time you have worked your way
through the text you should be able to handle
such material as:

---

*As well as many others.

1. The UNESCO Bulletin for Librarians
   (in Russian)
2. Novye Knigi (Russian weekly pre-pub-
lication list)
3. Knizhnaia Letopis'(Russian National
Bibliography)

In addition to serving the needs of the
librarian handling Russian materials, the
text should also serve the needs of the instructor wishing to present a concise course.
The material presented herein was completed
in 14 lectures. At the 15th a final examination was given comprising the following:

1. A vocabulary test
2. A series of questions in English to
be answered in English based on the student's
understanding of a reading taken from a Russian book or periodical dealing with librarianship. Students were permitted to use the
dictionary for this portion of the final examination.

The chief visual aid for this course
was an overhead projector used to reproduce
the assigned exercises. Each word was thus
analyzed - its definition, structure and
usage in a given context.

The course met with much success mea-
sured by the following criteria:

1. An overwhelming majority of students
were able to determine the main points in
the readings presented even though 98% had
never studied Russian before.
2. A number of students later reported
they had positions where they were success-
fully applying their knowledge of Russian
based on this course alone.

READING THE RUSSIAN LANGUAGE

CHAPTER I

To begin with, let me introduce you to
the complete Russian alphabet (Fig. 1).
Shown here are the following: the printed
form (capital and lower cases); the cursive
(italicized) form; the names of the Russian
letters; the transliterations as establish-
ed by the Library of Congress.

The printed form is most commonly used
in printed matter. But, the cursive must
also be learned since the librarian is often
faced with these characters in journals,
title pages of books, etc. (Fig. 2). This
form is also used to establish emphasis in
printed material (Fig. 3).

Learning the Printed Letter

In examining Fig. 1, it will be seen
that some letters are actually quite familiar in one way or another. For instance,
the following are pronounced like those in
the Latin alphabet:

Russian Letter	Pronounced as in
A	*car*
E*	*y*ell
К	*k*iss

---

*Pronunciation may vary slightly depending
on position in the Russian word.

Printed		Cursive	Letter Names	Translit-eration
А	а	*Аа*	ah	a
Б	б	*Бб*	beh	b
В	в	*Вв*	veh	v
Г	г	*Гг*	geh	g
Д	д	*Дд*	deh	d
Е	е	*Ее*	yeh	e
Ё	ё	*Ёё*	yaw	ё
Ж	ж	*Жж*	zheh	zh
З	з	*Зз*	zeh	z
И	и	*Ии*	ee	i
Й	й	*Йй*	ee kratkoye[1]	ĭ
К	к	*Кк*	kah	k
Л	л	*Лл*	el	l
М	м	*Мм*	em	m
Н	н	*Нн*	en	n
О	о	*Оо*	aw	o
П	п	*Пп*	peh	p
Р	р	*Рр*	ehr	r
С	с	*Сс*	ess	s
Т	т	*Тт*	teh	t

Figure I

THE RUSSIAN ALPHABET

[1] Short i.

Printed		Cursive	Letter Names	Translit-eration
У	у	*Уу*	*oo*	u
Ф	ф	*Фф*	*ef*	f
Х	х	*Хx*	*khah*	kh
Ц	ц	*Цц*	*tseh*	$\widehat{ts}$
Ч	ч	*Чч*	*cheh*	ch
Ш	ш	*Шш*	*shah*	sh
Щ	щ	*Щщ*	*shchah*	shch
	ъ	*ъ*	*tvyawrdy znak*1	"
	ы	*ы*	*yerih*	y
	ь	*ь*	*miakhky znak*2	'
Э	э	*Ээ*	*eh oborawt-noye*3	ė
Ю	ю	*Юю*	*yoo*	$\widehat{iu}$
Я	я	*Яя*	*yah*	$\widehat{ia}$

Figure I
(Continued)

THE RUSSIAN ALPHABET

1Hard sign (silent).
2Soft sign (silent).
3Reversed e.

Общественно-
политическая
литература

Figure 2

человéк?» — прибáвил Манѝлов. «Совершéнная прáвда, — сказáл Чѝчиков, — *препочтéннейший* человéк...» «А вѝце-губернáтор, не прáвда ли, какóй *мѝлый* человéк?» — сказáл Манѝлов... «Óчень, óчень *достóйный* человéк», — отвéтил Чѝчиков».

Figure 3

Russian Letter	Pronounced as in
М	*m*ake
О	p*o*rt
Т	*t*ime

Note that the following letters *look* like those in the Latin alphabet but are *pronounced* differently:

Russian Letter	Pronounced as in
В	*v*ent
Н	*n*ap
Р	*r*ow
С	*s*ing
У	l*oo*t

Other letters are derived from the Greek alphabet and again may be familiar to some:

Russian Letter	Pronounced as in
Б	*b*ake
Г	*g*o
Д	*d*ate
Л	*l*ove
П	*p*an

Russian Letter	Pronounced as in
Ф	*f*ull
Х	Ba*ch* (German)

Resembling somewhat letters in the Hebrew alphabet are the following:

Russian Letter	Pronounced as in
Ш	*sh*ake
Щ	fi*sh ch*ip
Ц	*ts*e*ts*e

The remaining letters must be newly learned by most:

Russian Letter	Pronounced as in
Е	*y*aw*n*
Ж	mea*s*ure
З	*z*ip
И	*e*vil
Й	da*y*
Ч	*ch*eck
Ъ	silent (used between two syllables)
Ы	*id*
Ь	silent (softens consonant it follows)

Russian Letter	Pronounced as in
Э	*e*lf
Ю	*u*nit
Я	*y*acht

Some Differences in the Cursive Form

The following cursive letters are some-times confusing since they differ in form from their corresponding printed letters:

Cursive	Printed	Transliterated
г	г	g
дg	д	d
п	п	p
т	т	t
ч	ч	ch

In the context of a word, these letters are written thus:

Cursive	Transliterated	English
академия	akademiia	academy
газета	gazeta	newspaper
паспорт	pasport	passport
литература	literatura	literature
часть	chast'	part

Learning the Order of the Alphabet

    To use the dictionary most efficiently,
it is of course, necessary to learn the order
of the Russian alphabet. There are 32 - or
33 letters if the Ё is included. The dieresis changes the sound as indicated in Fig. 1
but in using the dictionary it is treated as
though it were an Е. This does not hold
true for the Й which follows И in the dictionary and even appears on rare occasions
as the first letter of a word, e. g. ЙОД
(iodine). This letter is usually found after
a vowel as the second part of a diphthong.

    Basically, learning the alphabet is a
matter of memorization and as an aid, one
might use such mnemonic devices as saying -
ah, beh, veh, geh, deh, yeh, zheh, zeh, for
the first eight letters. Repeating aloud the
"locomotive series" - *khah, tseh, cheh, shah,
shchah,* for the Х, Ц, Ч, Ш, Щ, group of letters may be useful too. Difficulties also
seem to appear in remembering that between
the Russian А (a) and В (v) is the letter Б
(b) and that the Г (g) precedes the Д (d),
which is a reversal of the Latin alphabet.
The К (k), Л (l), М (m), Н (n), О (o), П (p),
and the Р (r), С (s), Т (t), У (u), groupings
are the same as in the Latin alphabet.

    The final five letters in the alphabet
may present a problem too in memorization.
The *hard* sign ъ resembles a musical note and
comes earlier than the *soft* sign ь just as
the word *hard* comes befcre the word *soft*
alphabetically, and both these letters have
the ы (y) between them.

    It will be noted when consulting the
dictionary that there are no words beginning

with the letters ъ, ы or ь; they appear in
other positions within and at the end of
words, e. g.

Russian	Transliterated	Pronounced	English
объём	ob"ём	*obyawm*	volume
анналы	annaly	*annaly**	annals
рубль	rubl'	*roobl*	ruble

The last three letters might be remem-
bered by saying the "hall*eluj*ah series" -
eh, yoo, yah for Э (e), Ю (iu) and Я (ia),
the last letter sounding almost like the
first letter of the Russian alphabet - A.

Why transliterate?

In order to make Russian literary material more accessible to the reader, the
Russian title must be interalphabetized with
the English title in the cataloging procedure. An accurate written transliteration
(replacing the Russian letters with their
English equivalents according to the Library
of Congress transliteration scheme) would
then be required.

Many technical and non-technical cog-
nate words become easily recognizable to the
reader in transliterated form too:

Russian	Transliterated	English
бюллетень	biulleten'	bulletin
альманах	al'manakh	almanac

*Pronounced shorter than the и (more like the
i in *it* - see page 6)

Russian	Transliterated	English
дисконт	diskont	discount
журнал	zhurnal	journal
каталог	katalog	catalog

Translation Pitfalls

Some Russian words, when transliterated, can occasionally be misleading. For example, these are familiar when transliterated but look at the actual meanings:

Russian	Transliterated	English
роман	roman	novel
фамилия	familiia	surname
магазин	magazin	store
лист	list	leaf
конверт	konvert	envelope

And, at first glance, these Russian words look exactly like English words, but have no relationship whatsoever:

Russian	Transliterated	English
том*	tom	volume
море	more	sea
то	to	than, then

*Not a synonym for объём (volume-amount).

Now, to restore your confidence, these look familiar when transliterated, and are completely trustworthy:

Russian	Transliterated	English
атом	atom	atom
акт	akt	act
Азия	Aziîa	Asia
текст	tekst	text
институт	institut	institute
профессор	professor	professor
телефон	telefon	telephone

Stressing Syllables

Although it is helpful to pronounce words after transliterating them, I do not feel it necessary to take up the subject of syllable stress. The library terms though, presented at the end of each chapter, *are* shown with stress signs so that at least *they* can be memorized with the proper emphasis.

Vocabulary *

академия	*(f)*	N	academy
альманах	*(m)*	N	almanac
анналы	*pl.*	N	annals
бюллетень	*(m)*	N	bulletin
газета	*(f)*	N	newspaper
дисконт	*(m)*	N	discount
журнал	*(m)*	N	journal
институт	*(m)*	N	institute
каталог	*(m)*	N	catalog
литература	*(f)*	N	literature
магазин	*(m)*	N	store
роман	*(m)*	N	novel
рубль	*(m)*	N	ruble

---

*Commonly used library terms introduced in
the chapter. Gender, parts of speech and
meanings are given. Plural number is noted
where applicable. Since many of these terms
are used in succeeding chapters, it is suggested that they be committed to memory.

EXERCISE

Alphabetize Each Group of Russian Letters:

I	II	III	IV	V	VI
Г	Д	Ч	Ж	Ю	*г*
Б	В	С	З	Щ	*д*
Ц	З	Ш	Г	Я	*т*
З	Э	У	Ф	Й	*м*
С	Б	Х	И	У	*п*

Transliterate:

1. схема
2. статья
3. рубль
4. объяснять
5. вы
6. эпоха
7. сложный
8. тысяча
9. филолог
10. улица
11. ещё
12. *знан*

13. *брошюра*

How would you write the following names in
English? First transliterate – then guess:

1. Вашингтон
2. Дьюи
3. Хрущёв
4. Нью Йорк
5. Вьетнам

CHAPTER 2

Definite and Indefinite Articles

The first important point to remember is that in Russian, there are no definite or indefinite articles. It is up to the reader to choose which fits best in the context of a sentence, or whether it is necessary at all. An example is the following book title:

Теория Математических Машин

or transliterated:

Teoriia Matematicheskikh Mashin

A guess with regard to the translation might lead to:

Theory Mathematical Machine

Another word order would lead to:

Mathematical Machine Theory

With the addition of the definite or indefinite article in an appropriate location:

The Mathematical Machine Theory

or

A Mathematical Machine Theory

Another example is the book title

Машинные Техники

which is transliterated to

Mashinnye Tekhniki

Again, we seem to have another form of the word *machine*, and the next word appears to be *technique*. This title could be

Machine Technique

The *Machine Technique*

A *Machine Technique*

Machine Techniques

Another example is

Библиотеки В Америки

which is transliterated to

Biblioteki v Ameriki

A shrewd guess would suggest that *biblioteki* means *library* and of course, *Ameriki* is *America*. But, the transliteration of В to v in no way suggests its meaning. It would be necessary to consult a dictionary to determine that it is a word in itself* and that its most common meaning is *in*. The title could then be translated, alternatively, as

Libraries in America

---

*As are the letters а, и, к, о, с, у and я.

The *Library in America*

A *Library in America*

Libraries in the *Americas*

Working with the Dictionary

The sequence of the alphabet was cover-
ed in Chapter 1, and you are now ready to
venture into the use of a Russian-English
dictionary. The dictionary chosen in con-
nection with this textbook* is

B. A. Lapidus and S. V. Shevtsova,
*The Learner's Russian-English
Dictionary*, The M.I.T. Press, Massa-
chusetts Institute of Technology,
Cambridge, Massachusetts

Let us start with the translation of
nouns. Nouns appear in the dictionary in
the singular, nominative case of either the
masculine, feminine or neuter gender. The
stem of the noun is distinguished from the
rest of the word in this manner:

теори|я

машин|а

Some words are found in the dictionary
exactly as they appear in print, e. g.
теория appears as_

теори|я *f* -и, -й theory

---

*All definitions used are quoted directly
 from this dictionary with the permission of
 the copyright owner.

   Others do not appear in the same form
in the dictionary. The stems may be the
same but the inflections (endings following
the stem) may differ, e. g. машин appears as

       машин│а *f* -ы, ~ 1. machine,
       mechanism; engine;

The definition for машина (apparently related to машин) may thus be used in translation.

   The *f* designates the gender of машина -
feminine. The letter ы following the gender
designation signifies that машина may appear
as машины. The sign ~ indicates that the
stem may also be used with no ending (машин).
The basic meaning for this word is still
machine, but the various endings reflect
different cases of the noun. This will be
discussed in more detail in Chapter 3.

   An adjective appears in the dictionary
in the singular, nominative case and always
in the masculine gender. Take, for example,
the Russian adjective логический:

       логическ│ий *a* -ая, -ое, -ие
       logical (*approach, result,
       etc.*).

   Following the designation *a*, for adjective, are three different endings for the
stem логическ indicating that this adjective
may also appear as логическая, логическое
and логические.

   Adjectives, verbs and pronouns, like
nouns, may also appear in a sentence with
other endings than those shown in the dictionary. This depends on their function in
the sentence. The other parts of speech -

adverbs, conjunctions, prepositions, etc., are unchanging and only appear in print as they are shown in the dictionary.

Adjective Identification

In English, a noun can serve as an adjective in modifying another noun as in - *university* library, with no change in the word. On the other hand, in Russian, the adjective in this case - *university*, would acquire a changed ending.

As an aid to identifying a part of speech as being either a noun or an adjective, here are a few examples to refer to when translating:

Noun	Adjective
университет *university*	университет<u>ский</u> *university*
библиотека *library*	библиоте<u>чный</u> *library*
библиография *bibliography*	библиографи<u>чиский</u> *bibliographic*
информация *information*	информаци<u>онный</u> *information*
автор *author*	автор<u>ский</u> *author*
читатель *reader*	читатель<u>ный</u> *reader*

*Converting Letter Sounds from One Language
  to Another*

In comparing the Latin and Russian alphabet, there are many letters in the Latin
alphabet which do not appear at all in the
Russian. The chart in Figure 4 will be
most helpful in determining how these and
other letters are converted from one language to the other. This will be particu-
larly useful to the librarian in decoding
proper names.

Idioms

It will probably come as no surprise
that idiomatic expressions are to be found
in the Russian language. This will be
evidenced by a series of words which, when
translated, seem to have no meaning. For
example:

Что такое литература?

The dictionary definition of Что is:

что *pron* чего, чему,
~, чем, (о) чём 1. *in-
ter & rel* what;

The dictionary definition of такое is:

так|ой *pron dem & def*
-ая, -ое, -ие 1. such;

The last word is transliterated as - *liter-
atura*. Even without consulting the dictionary, we can guess confidently that it means-
literature. Putting together the English
definitions produces:

Figure 4 - Conversion of Letters

Russian	Transliteration	English	Explanation
автор	avtor	author	Russian ав replaces English au and the т - the th.
Ейзенхауер	Ĕizenkhauer	Eisenhower	Russian ей is transliterated to ei. The Russian з replaces the English s. Russian х replaces English h and the Russian ау replaces (phonetically) English ow.
Максвелл	Maksvell	Maxwell	The Russian кс replaces English x and в replaces English w.
Гамбург	Gamburg	Hamburg	In this case the Russian г replaces the English h.
Гавана	Gavana	Havana	See above.
Джонс	Dzhons	Jones	The дж sound replaces the J.

Figure 4 continued on next page

Figure 4 (continued)

Russian	Transliteration	English	Explanation
Иордан	Iordan	Jordan	The Russian И may also replace the English J.
Куба	Kuba	Cuba	The Russian К always replaces this type of C.
Квебек	Kvebek	Quebec	The Russian Кв replaces English qu.
Оксфорд	Oksford	Oxford	A further illustration of the Russian кс replacing English x.
Саутгемптон	Sautgempton	Southhampton	The Russian т replaces the English th, the г - the h, and the е - the a.
логарифм	logarifm	logarithm	In this case, the Russian ф replaces English th.
Ханой	Khanoi	Hanoi	The Russian Х may also replace the English H.

Уодсуорт *Uodsuort* Wadsworth The Russian у replaces the English w, the т - the th.

Цейлон *T͡seĭlon* Ceylon The Russian Ц replaces the English C in this case.

Ейнштейн *Eĭnshteĭn* Einstein The Russian spelling here seems to literally follow the English except for the Ш replacing the s.

What such literature?

which obviously makes no sense. But looking
further in the dictionary under токой, we
find:

> что ~ое..?: что ~ое "го-
> родки"? what is "gorodki"?

Thus, when the two words что такое are
used together, they mean *what is*, and

> Что такое литература?

is translated as

> *What is literature?*

A Practice Translation

You should now be ready to try your
hand at translating a Table of Contents using the dictionary* and applying the few
rules introduced thus far.

In Figure 5 is a segment of a contents
page of a Russian journal listing author
names and titles of articles. Space has
been provided so that you may enter first
the transliteration. The next step is to
translate either by attempting to guess
those words which may be recognized after
transliteration or by consulting the dictionary for words which you do not recognize.

After you have done as well as you can

---

* As an additional aid, a list of Commonly
Used Library Terms and Abbreviations has
been provided (Pages 213 ff.)

on your own, you may check your work against
the transliteration and translation in Figure 6 on pages 28-31.

A PRACTICE TRANSLATION

Figure 5

Содержание

Н. И. Тюлина. Национальная библиотека.

Современные проблемы обслуживания

О. И. Глобачев. Научная и техническая

документация и информация в Республике

В библиотеках Финляндии

Э. И. Лесохина и Т. П. Пышнова.

Н. Б. Медведева. Библиотечное обслуживание

М. Надворник и Б. Смейкал. Государственная

Figure 5 (continued)

Figure 6

TRANSLITERATION AND TRANSLATION
OF CONTENTS PAGE IN FIGURE 5

Содержание[1]
Soderzhanie
Contents

Н. И. Тюлина.   Национальная* библиотека.
N. I. Tiulina. Natsional'naia biblioteka.
N. I. Tiulina.   National   library.

Современные[2] проблемы* обслуживания[3]
Sovremennye problemy obsluzhivaniia
Modern   problem   service

читателей[4]
chitatelei
reader

---

[1] содержа́ние *(n)* N contents

[2] совреме́нн|ый *a sh.f* совремeн, -а, -о, -ы
1. contemporary (*literature, etc*); ~ое
положе́ние present situation; 2. modern, up-
to-date.

[3] обслу́живание *n* -я, -й 1. service (*in a rest-
aurant, hotel, etc; medical, etc*); 2. main-
tenance, servicing (*of cars, etc*).

[4] чита́тель *(m)* N reader

*The definitions given for words marked with
an asterisk have been guessed from the
transliteration.

Figure 6 (continued)

О. И. Глобачев.   Научная[1] и[2] техническая*
O. I. Globachev. Nauchnaia i tekhnicheskaia
O. I. Globachev. Scientific and   technical

документация*   и   информация* в[3]Республике*
dokumentatsiia i informatsiia v Respublike
documentation and information in Republic

Куба*
Kuba
Cuba

В   библиотеках   Финляндии*
V bibliotekakh Finliandii
In   library   Finland

Э. И. Лесохина   и Т. П. Пышнова
E. I. Lesokhina i T. P. Pyshnova
E. I. Lesokhina and T. P. Pyshnova

Университетские*библиотеки
Universitetskie biblioteki
    University   library

---

*The definitions given for words marked with
an asterisk have been guessed from the
transliteration.

[1] нау́чн|ый *a sh f* научен, -а, -о, -ы scientif-
ic.

[2] и *I cj denoting 1. connexion, addition* and;
and then; я и он he and I;

[3] ь, во *prep...II with pr denoting 1. position
inside of, within:* в комнате in the room;

Н. Б. Медведева. Библиотечное[1] обслуживание
N. B. Medvedeva. Bibliotechnoe obsluzhivanie
N. B. Medvedeva.   Library   service

детей[2]
detei
children

М. Надворник и Б. Смейкал. Государственная[3]
M. Nadvornik i B. Smeikal. Gosudarstvennaia
M. Nadvornik and B. Smeikal.   State

  научная библиотека в Оломоуце.* 1566-1966
  nauchnaia biblioteka v Olomoufse.1566-1966
  scientific library   in Olomouc. 1566-1966

  ИЗ[4] МЕЖДУНАРОДНОЙ[5] БИБЛИОТЕЧНОЙ ЖИЗНИ[6]
  IZ MEZHDUNARODNOI BIBLIOTECHNOI ZHIZNI
  FROM INTERNATIONAL   LIBRARY   LIFE

---

*The definitions given for words marked with
an asterisk have been guessed from the
transliteration.

[1] библиоте́чный Adj. library

[2] де́т|и *pl* -ей, -ям, -ей, -ьми, (о) -ях *(sing*
дитя *n)* children.

[3] госуда́рственн|ый *a* state; national..;

[4] из, изо...*prep with gen denoting*...2. *a*
source of information,etc: узнать из газет
learn from the papers;

[5] междунаро́дный *a* international.

[6] жизн|ь *f* -ей life;

Figure 6 (continued)

Международное   совещание[1] европейских[2]
Mezhdunarodnoe soveshchanie evropeiskikh
International   conference   European

социалистических* стран[3] по[4]вопросам[5]
sofsialisticheskikh   stran   po voprosam
Socialistic   country on question

координации* комплектования[6] библиотек
koordinafsii komplektovaniia bibliotek
coordination   acquisition   library

(Прага,* 6-8 апреля* 1965 г.[7])
(Praga,   6-8 aprelia 1965 g.)
(Prague, 6-8 April   1965   )

---

[1] совеща́ни|е *n* -я, -й conference, meeting...

[2] европе́йск|ий *a* -ая, -ое, -ие European.

[3] стран|а́ *f* -ы, *pl* страны,~1.country...

[4] по *prep*...7. *a field, sphere of activity:*
...лекция по вопросу о...a lecture on the
problem of...

[5] вопро́с *m* -а, -ов question...

[6] комплектова́ние *(n)* N acquisition

[7] The abbreviation for год (translated as
year) customarily follows when a year is
mentioned. It is to be ignored in translation.

*The definitions given for words marked with
an asterisk have been guessed from the
transliteration.

Vocabulary

библиогра́фия	*(f)*	N	bibliography
библиоте́ка	*(f)*	N	library
библиоте́чный		Adj.	library
госуда́рственный		Adj.	state
информа́ция	*(f)*	N	information
комплектова́ние	*(n)*	N	acquisition
междунаро́дный		Adj.	international
нау́ка	*(f)*	N	science
нау́чный		Adj.	scientific
обслу́живание	*(n)*	N	service
совеща́ние	*(n)*	N	conference
университе́т	*(m)*	N	university
чита́тель	*(m)*	N	reader

EXERCISE

*Translate these Titles with the Use of the
  Dictionary:*

  1. Информация в Области Биологии

  2. Международный Обмен Медицинской
      Литературы

  3. Машинный Перевод

*How would you write the following names in
  English? First transliterate - then guess:*

  1. Хемингуей
  2. О Хара
  3. Австралия
  4. Гомер
  5. Уитман
  6. Свифт

CHAPTER 3

Nouns

Russian noun declensions have six cases.
A noun appears in the dictionary in the nominative, singular case. A change in the
case of the noun will affect the ending of
the noun.

Figure 7 explains the use of the **six**
cases and the changes the noun том (*volume*)
undergoes.

There are other nouns of the masculine
gender, which in the nominative, singular
case end in (1) a consonant, (2) the letter
ь, or (3) the letter й. Figure 8 shows the
declensions of some typical nouns of the
masculine gender.

Another group of masculine nouns, ending with a consonant is declined somewhat
differently. An example is the following:

доктор (*doctor*)

Case	Stem of noun	Endings Sing-ular	Plu-ral
Nominative (N)	доктор		а
Genitive (G)	"	а	ов
Dative (D)	"	у	ам
Accusative (A)	"	а	ов
Instrumental (I)	"	ом	ами
Prepositional (P)	"	е	ах

Figure 7 - Explanation of Declensions

NOUN	CASE	EXPRESSES	ANSWERS	TRANSLATED AS IN
том	nominative	subject	who, what	*The volume* is large.
том<u>а</u>	genitive	possession	Of whom, of what	Part *of the volume* is completed.
том<u>у</u>	dative	indirect object	To whom, to what	I am adding *to the volume.*
том	accusative	direct object	Whom, what	I am using *the volume.*
том<u>ом</u>	instrumental	agent or instrument	By whom, what, with whom, what	The set was completed *with the volume.*
том<u>е</u>	prepositional*	location, concerning	Where, about whom, about what	The chapter is in *the volume.*

*The noun in this case is always preceded by a preposition.

Figure 8 – Declension of Masculine Nouns

том (*volume*)

Case	Stem of noun	Endings Singular	Endings Plural
N	том		ы
G	=	а	ов
D	=	у	ам
A	=		ы
I	=	ом	ами
P	=	е	ах

знак (*sign*)

Case	Stem of noun	Endings Singular	Endings Plural
N	знак		и
G	=	а	ов
D	=	у	ам
A	=		и
I	=	ом	ами
P	=	е	ах

указатель (*index*)

Case	Stem of noun	Endings Singular	Endings Plural
N	указател	ь	и
G	=	я	ей
D	=	ю	ям
A	=	ь	и
I	=	ем	ями
P	=	е	ях

случай (*case*)

Case	Stem of noun	Endings Singular	Endings Plural
N	случа	й	и
G	=	я	ев
D	=	ю	ям
A	=	й	и
I	=	ем	ями
P	=	е	ях

It should be noted that unlike the other masculine nouns in Figure 8, доктор is animate. In declensions of animate nouns agreement is indicated between the Genitive and Accusative singular and plural cases, whereas declensions of inanimate nouns show agreement between the Nominative and Accusative singular and plural cases.

Shown in Figure 9 are some typical feminine nouns and their scheme of endings.

Some typical neuter noun declensions are:

общество (*society*)

Case	Stem of noun	Endings Singular	Endings Plural
N	обществ	о	а
G	"	а	
D	"	у	ам
A	"	о	а
I	"	ом	ами
P	"	е	ах

описание (*entry*)

Case	Stem of noun	Endings Singular	Endings Plural
N	описани	е	я
G	"	я	й
D	"	ю	ям
A	"	е	я
I	"	ем	ямй
P	"	и	ях

Figure 9 – Declension of Feminine Nouns

наука (*science*)

Case	Stem of noun	Endings	
		Sing-ular	Plu-ral
N	наук	а	и
G	=	и	
D	=	е	ам
A	=	у	и
I	=	ой	ами
P	=	е	ах

школа (*school*)

Case	Stem of noun	Endings	
		Sing-ular	Plu-ral
N	школ	а	ы
G	=	ы	
D	=	е	ам
A	=	у	ы
I	=	ой	ами
P	=	е	ах

теория (*theory*)

Case	Stem of noun	Endings	
		Sing-ular	Plu-ral
N	теори	я	и
G	=	и	й
D	=	и	ям
A	=	ю	й
I	=	ей	ями
P	=	и	ях

часть (*part*)

Case	Stem of noun	Endings	
		Sing-ular	Plu-ral
N	част	ь	и
G	=	и	ей
D	=	и	ям
A	=	ь	и
I	=	ью	ями
P	=	и	ях

In addition to the typical declensions shown, there are many other irregularly declined nouns*.

As can be seen from the typical noun declensions, all Russian noun endings begin with a vowel. The vowels in the Russian alphabet are referred to as *hard* and *soft* - the distinction being as follows:

Hard Vowel	Pronounced	Soft Vowel	Pronounced
а	ah	я	yah
э	eh	е	yeh
ы	iy	и	yiy
о	aw	ё	yaw
у	oo	ю	yoo

Further examination of the endings indicates that similar sounding hard and soft vowels such as а (ah) and я (yah) are initial letters of endings of the same cases of different genders of nouns, e.g.:

Noun	Dative Plural	Instrumental Plural	Prepositional Plural
том (Masc.)	том<u>а</u>м	том<u>а</u>ми	том<u>а</u>х
случай (Masc.)	случа<u>я</u>м	случа<u>я</u>ми	случа<u>я</u>х
книга (Fem.)	книг<u>а</u>м	книг<u>а</u>ми	книг<u>а</u>х
общество (Neut.)	обществ<u>а</u>м	обществ<u>а</u>ми	обществ<u>а</u>х

*See B. A. Lapidus and S. V. Shevtsova, *The Learner's Russian-English Dictionary*, The M.I.T. Press, Massachusetts Institute of Technology, Cambridge, Massachusetts, pp. 551-577. (1963)

It is helpful to know that ам or ям
are always endings of the Dative plural
case, ами or ями are always endings of the
Instrumental plural case and ах or ях are
always endings of the Prepositional plural
case.

Figure 10 presents all noun endings in
alphabetical sequence and identifies the
possible gender (s), cases and number.

Let us go through an exercise of translating the noun

библиотеках

using the dictionary, Figure 10 and our
knowledge of noun declensions. The dictionary entry

библиотек|а *f* -и, ~ library;

shows the stem to be библиотек *-* the ending
then, is ах. Since all endings of ах or ях
are the Prepositional plural case, this ending is found in Figure 10 under all genders.
A noun in the Prepositional case must be
preceded by a preposition. If the preposition were в the two words would mean -
in (the) libraries.

In translating the noun

библиотекарей

the dictionary entry

библиотекар|ь *m* -я, -ей librarian.

indicates that this word is of the Masculine
gender and ends in the letter ь. Also, this

*Following the gender designation are the
endings for Genitive singular and plural cases.

FIGURE 10

NOUN ENDINGS

Abbreviations: N-*Nominative;* G-*Genitive;*
D-*Dative;* A-*Accusative;* I-*Instrumental;*
P-*Prepositional;* s-*singular;* pl-*plural;*
in.-*inanimate;* an.-*animate (all other endings are for inanimate and animate nouns)*

	Masculine	Feminine	Neuter
-*	Ns	Gpl, Apl an.	Gpl
а	Gs, As an., Npl, Apl in.	Ns	Gs,Npl,Apl
ам	Dpl	Dpl	Dpl
ами	Ipl	Ipl	Ipl
ах	Ppl	Ppl	Ppl
е	Ps	Ds, Ps	Ns,As,Ps
ев	Gpl, Apl an.		Gpl
ёв	Gpl, Apl an.		
ей	Gpl, Apl an.	Is, Gpl	Gpl
ем	Is		Is
и	Ps, Npl, Apl in.	Gs, Ds, Ps, Npl, Apl in.	Ps
й	Ns, As, Npl, Apl	Gpl	Gpl

*No ending beyond the stem of the noun.

	Masculine	Feminine	Neuter
о			Ns, As
ов	Gpl, Apl an.		
ой		Is	
ом	Is		Is
ою	Ds	Is	
у	Ds	As	Ds
ы	Npl, Apl in.	Gs, Npl, Apl in.	
ь	Ns, As in.	Ns, As, Gpl, Apl an.	
ю	Ds	As	Ds
я	Gs, As an., Npl, Apl in.	Ns	Gs, Npl, Apl
ям	Dpl	Dpl	Dpl
ями	Ipl	Ipl	Ipl
ях	Ppl	Ppl	Ppl

is an animate noun. The stem is библиотекар.
Figure 10 shows the ending ей for masculine
animate nouns as being either Genitive plural
or Accusative plural cases, depending on the
context of the sentence in which the noun
appears. Then translation then, is - *of
librarians* (Genitive plural) - or - *librarians* (Accusative plural).

For the noun

книгой

the dictionary entry

книг|а *f* -и, ~ book

indicates that this is a feminine noun with
the stem книг. The ending ой under the feminine gender column in Figure 10, is denoted
as the Instrumental singular case. The noun
then, is translated as - *by the (a) book* -
or - *with the (a) book* (Instrumental singular
case).

Prepositions

The case of a noun depends not only on
its position in a sentence but also on
whether the noun is preceded by a preposition.
The preposition then, will determine the case
of the noun. Take, for example, the preposition без (without). The noun which follows
this word will appear in the Genitive case
only because без governs that case. Thus,

без книги

is translated as *without the (a) book*, whereas if книги stood alone, the ending и for a

feminine noun would indicate not only the
Genitive singular case but the Dative singular, the Prepositional singular, the Nominative plural or the Accusative plural cases
as well. книги would then be translated depending on the context of the sentence in
which it appeared.

   Another example is

          между библиотеками

The noun which follows the preposition между
(between) is in the Instrumental plural case.
The translation of the phrase is *between (the)*
libraries. In other words, библиотеками is
not being translated as *by (the) libraries*
or *with (the) libraries* as the Instrumental
case ending would indicate if there were no
preposition preceding it.

   Figure 11 lists alphabetically the most
common prepositions, their meanings and the
case (cases) each one governs. It should be
noted from Figure 11 that sometimes the noun
following a preposition is in one case and
at other times - a different case. The meaning of the preposition may vary depending on
what the case of the noun may be.

A Practice Translation

   In Figure 12 is a segment of a contents
page of a Russian book. Space has been provided so that you may enter the transliteration and translation based on your present
knowledge. You may check your work against
the transliteration and translation in Figure 13 on pages 50 - 55.

Figure II - Prepositions

	Genitive	Dative	Accusative	Instrumental	Prepositional
без	without				
близ	near				
в(о)			into, in, to		in
вдоль	along				
вместо	instead of				
вне	outside				
внутри	within				
возле	near, beside				
вокруг	around				
для	for				
до	up to, until				
за			for	behind, beyond, for, after	
из	out of, from, of				
из-за	from behind, because of				
к		toward, to			
кроме	besides, except				

	Genitive	Dative	Accusative	Instrumental	Prepositional
между				among, between	
мимо	past				
на			onto, to, on, for		on, in, at
над(о)				over, above	
о(б)			against		about
около	near,				
от	away from, from				
перед				in front of, before	
по		along, over, according to, on	for		after
под			under	under, near	
позади	behind				
после	afterwards				
посреди	amidst				
прежде	before				
при					at, near, in the presence of, during
про			about		

Figure 11 continued on next page

FIGURE II (continued)

	Genitive	Dative	Accusative	Instrumental	Prepositional
против	against				
ради	for the sake of				
с(о)	from, since		about, approximately	with, along with	
сверх	over				
сквозь			through		
у	by, at, near, in, next to				
через			across, over, through, by		

FIGURE 12

OГЛАВЛЕНИЕ

Figure 13

TRANSLITERATION AND TRANSLATION
OF CONTENTS PAGE IN FIGURE 12

Оглавление[1]
Oglavlenie
Table of Contents

Предисловие[2] от[3] автора[4]
Predislovie   ot   avtora
Preface from author

 Глава[5] I
 Glava I
Chapter I

---

[1]оглавлени|е *(n)* N Table of contents

[2]предислови|е *(n)* N preface, introduction

[3]Figure 11 indicates that this preposition
means *from* and governs the Genitive case.

[4]автор *m* -а, -ов author
 Appears above in the Genitive case because
 of the preposition preceding.

[5]глав|а *(f)* N chapter

Вычислительные[1]   машины   и   выбор[2]
Vychislitel'nye mashiny   i   vybor
  Calculating   machines and choice

    решения[3]
    resheniia
  of decision

---

[1]This word does not have a noun ending. It
is not listed in the dictionary but the
stem shown in this dictionary entry

вычисл|ять ....calculate, compute

is the same. Since the noun following —
(машины) is probably the Nominative plural
case, we can guess that вычислительные
means *calculating* or *computing*.

[2]выбор *m* -а 1. choice

[3]решени|е *n* -я, -й 1. decision
Figure 10 indicates that the я ending for a
neuter noun may be Genitive singular, nominative plural or Accusative plural cases.
With the noun *choice* preceding this word,
selecting the Genitive singular case would
make best sense.

Figure 13 (continued)

Проблема*   информации[1]
Problema   informatsii
Problem   of   information

Глава   II
Glava   II
Chapter II

Введение[2]
Vvedenie
Introduction

---

*The definitions given for words marked with an asterisk have been guessed from the transliteration.

[1]Although the meaning can be guessed from transliteration, it is necessary to know the dictionary entry in order to determine the gender and case of the noun:

информаци|я *f* -и, -й 1. information

Figure 11 indicates that the и ending for feminine nouns could be applied to more than one case, but the Genitive singular seems to fit best in the context of the sentence.

[2]введени|е *(n)* N preface, introduction

Контроль*за[1] терминологией   и   предметными[2]
Kontrol' za terminologiei i predmetnymi
Control for terminology and subject

рубриками[3]
rubrikami
headings

---

*The definitions given for words marked with
an asterisk have been guessed from the
transliteration.

[1]Figure 11 indicates that this preposition
governs the Accusative or Instrumental cases.
In examining the noun which follows

терминологи|я *(f)* N terminology

we find that the ей ending for feminine
nouns may be Genitive plural or Instrumental singular cases. It can then be safely
assumed that терминологией governed by за
is in the Instrumental singular case and
that the best meaning for за is *for*.

[2]This word does not have a noun ending. It
is not listed in the dictionary but the
stem shown in this dictionary entry

предмет *m* -а, -ов 2.subject

is the same. The second meaning seems to
fit best in the context.

[3]рубрик|а *(f)* N heading
Since this word is a part of the phrase
beginning with the preposition за, it is
also governed by за and appears in the
Instrumental (plural) case.

Figure 13 (continued)

Хранение[1] оригиналов[2]   документов,[2]
Khranenie originalov   dokumentov,
Storage of originals of documents,

выдержек,[3]   рефератов,[4]
vyderzhek,   referatov,
of excerpts, of abstracts,

---

[1]хранени|е *n* -я keeping, custody;...storage

[2]The meaning may be guessed from transliteration. The ов ending is Genitive plural.

[3]The dictionary entries,

выдержк|а *f* -и 1.self-control...2......

выдерж|ка *f* -ки, -ек   quotation, excerpt.

show two words spelled the same way. The meaning of the second entry not only makes more sense in context, but also shows the irregular ек ending as the Genitive plural.

[4]Before you are misled into thinking that this word means *reference,*

реферат *(m)* N abstract

The ов ending is Genitive plural for masculine nouns.

библиографических[1] описаний.[2]
bibliograficheskikh opisanii.
of bibliographic   entries.

---

[1]Transliteration suggests that this word has
to do with *bibliography*. Since it does not
have a noun ending, we can assume that it
is an adjective form and will be followed
by a noun.

[2]описани|е *(n)* N entry
Figure 10 shows the й ending as being
Genitive plural for a neuter noun.

Vocabulary

библиографический	Adj.	bibliographic
введéние *(n)*	N	introduction
вы́держка *(f)*	N	excerpt
главá *(f)*	N	chapter
óбщество *(n)*	N	society
оглавлéние *(n)*	N	table of contents
описáние *(n)*	N	entry
предислóвие *(n)*	N	introduction
реферáт *(m)*	N	abstract
ру́брика *(f)*	N	heading
том *(m)*	N	volume
часть *(f)*	N	part

EXERCISE

Using the dictionary and Figure 10, find the gender and case(s) of the following nouns:

1. реферате
2. рубрик
3. письма
4. издания
5. выпуску
6. картину
7. бумагой
8. отделении

VOCABULARY TEST
Give the meaning of the following words:

1. магазин
2. роман
3. газета
4. наука
5. обслуживание
6. государственный
7. комплектование
8. совещание
9. читатель
10. международный

CHAPTER 4

*Attributive Adjectives**

Adjectives appear in the dictionary in
the masculine, nominative, singular case.
Like nouns, they have different endings which
depend on the gender, case and number of the
noun being described. Figure 14 shows the
patterns of adjective declensions.

It may be confusing to note that, although some adjective endings (ой, ей, ом,
ем) are the same as noun endings, the cases
are not the same for nouns and adjectives.
Accordingly, it is necessary to consult the
dictionary to differentiate between the two
parts of speech. Examples of nouns and adjectives with identical endings are:

наук|ой	Noun	Instrumental
русск|ой	Adjective	Genitive,Dative, Instrumental, Prepositional
теори|ей	Noun	Instrumental
средн|ей	Adjective	Genitive,Dative, Instrumental, Prepositional
обществ|ом	Noun	Instrumental
русск|ом	Adjective	Prepositional
описани|ем	Noun	Instrumental
средн|ем	Adjective	Prepositional

*These adjectives generally precede the noun
 being modified; they are also known as long
 form adjectives.

Figure 14 - Declension of Adjectives

новый *(new)*

Case	Stem of Adjective	Endings Singular M	F	N	Plural
N	нов	ый	ая	ое	ые
G	"	ого*	ой	ого*	ых
D	"	ому	ой	ому	ым
A	"	ый	ую	ое	ые
I	"	ым	ой	ым	ыми
P	"	ом	ой	ом	ых

второй *(second)*

Case	Stem of Adjective	Endings Singular M	F	N	Plural
N	втор	ой	ая	ое	ые
G	"	ого*	ой	ого*	ых
D	"	ому	ой	ому	ым
A	"	ой	ую	ое	ые
I	"	ым	ой	ым	ыми
P	"	ом	ой	ом	ых

*Pronounced as though it were spelled ово.

русский *(Russian)*

Case	Stem of Adjective	Endings			
		Singular			Plural
		M	F	N	
N	русск	ий	ая	ое	ие
G	"	ого	ой	ого	их
D	"	ому	ой	ому	им
A	"	ий	ую	ое	ие
I	"	им	ой	им	ими
P	"	ом	ой	ом	их

средний *(medium)*

Case	Stem of Adjective	Endings			
		Singular			Plural
		M	F	N	
N	средн	ий	яя	ее	ие
G	"	его*	ей	его*	их
D	"	ему	ей	ему	им
A	"	ий	юю	ее	ие
I	"	им	ей	им	ими
P	"	ем	ей	ем	их

хороший *(good)*

Case	Stem of Adjective	Endings			
		Singular			Plural
		M	F	N	
N	хорош	ий	ая	ее	ие
G	"	его*	ей	его*	их
D	"	ему	ей	ему	им
A	"	ий	ую	ее	ие
I	"	им	ей	им	ими
P	"	ем	ей	ем	их

*Pronounced as though it were spelled ево.

Adjective and Noun Agreement

As in many other languages, adjectives and the nouns they modify must, in Russian, agree in gender, number and case. Some examples are:

	Gender	Number	Case(s)
нов|ыми том|ами	Masculine	Plural	I
втор|ой част|и	Feminine	Singular	G,D,P
средн|яя школ|а	Feminine	Singular	N
нов|ой наук|е	Feminine	Singular	D,P
нов|ых наук|ах	Feminine	Plural	P
русск|ому доктор|у	Masculine	Singular	D
русск|их обществ|	Neuter	Plural	G
хорош|ее описани|е	Neuter	Singular	N,A

Figure 15 presents all adjective endings in alphabetical sequence and identifies the possible gender(s), number and cases.

Proper Nouns

Like nouns and adjectives, names appearing in the context of a sentence will be shown with appropriate endings depending on their gender, number and case.

When translating a name into English, it must be returned to the nominative case if it is shown with another case ending.

The declensional pattern of a proper noun changes, depending on its final letters as shown in the nominative case. For example, if a masculine name in the nominative case ends in the letters ин, ын, ов, ев, ёв, it will retain those final letters in declension.

Figure 15

ADJECTIVE ENDINGS

Abbreviations: N-*Nominative;* G-*Genitive;*
D-*Dative;* A-*Accusative;* I-*Instrumental;*
P-*Prepositional;* in.-*inanimate;* an.-
*animate (all other endings apply to all
adjectives)*

	Singular			Plural
	Masculine	Feminine	Neuter	
ая		N		
его	G, A an.		G	
ее			N, A	
ей		G, D, I, P		
ем	P		P	
ему	D		D	
ие				N, A in.
ий	N, A in.			
им	I		I	D
ими				I
их				G, A an., P
ого	G, A an.		G	
ое			N, A	
ой	N, A in.	G, D, I, P		
ом	P		P	
ому	D		D	
ую		A		
ые				N, A in.
ый	N, A in.			
ым	I		I	D
ыми				I
ых				G, A an., P
юю		A		
яя		N		

Case endings are added as follows:

        N   Гагарин
        G   Гагарин а
        D   Гагарин у
        A   Гагарин а
        I   Гагарин ым
        P   Гагарин е

    The feminine and plural counterparts of
the same name are declined as follows:

               Feminine   Plural
        N   Гагарин а   Гагарин ы
        G   Гагарин ой   Гагарин ых
        D   Гагарин ой   Гагарин ым
        A   Гагарин у   Гагарин ых
        I   Гагарин ой   Гагарин ыми
        P   Гагарин ой   Гагарин ых

    Note that names ending with the letters
ин, ын, ов, ев, ёв, in the masculine, nominative case become feminine with the addition of the letter а in the nominative case.
On a catalog card, the feminine name would
be shown with this additional letter and
would be transliterated as (*Gagarina*).

    Names which in the masculine,nominative
case end in the letters ский are declined in
this manner:

        N   Нижинск ий
        G   Нижинск ого
        D   Нижинск ому
        A   Нижинск ого
        I   Нижинск им
        P   Нижинск ом

    Here, the feminine and plural counter-
parts of the same name are declined somewhat
differently:

	Feminine	Plural
N	Нижинск ая	Нижинск ие
G	Нижинск ой	Нижинск их
D	Нижинск ой	Нижинск им
A	Нижинск ую	Нижинск их
I	Нижинск ой	Нижинск ими
P	Нижинск ой	Нижинск их

Note here, that for declensional purposes, only the stem Нижинск is retained in
names ending with the letters ский in the
masculine, nominative case. A name of this
type becomes feminine with the addition of
the letters ая to the stem. On a catalog
card, the feminine name would be shown with
these additional letters and would be transliterated as *Nizhinskaia*.

In other words, women's names are
spelled differently from those of men in
their family; for cataloging purposes, this
difference is retained.*

Here are some general guidelines on the
declension of Russian names which end in
letters other than those shown above,in the
nominative case.

1. Masculine names ending in a
consonant in the nominative case,
with the exception of the letter
combinations ин, ын, ов, ев, ёв,
will be declined like the masculine, animate noun доктор (see
page 35).

Example: Маркс

---

*The name of Stalin's daughter, an authoress,
is cataloged under Stalina.

2. Names ending in the letter а
in the nominative case, with the
exception of the letter combinations ина, ына, ова, ева, ёва,
will be declined like feminine
nouns of the same type shown in
Figure 9.

Example: Волга

3. Names ending in the letters
е, и, о, у, in the nominative
case will appear undeclined.

Example: Евтушенко

4. Names of non-Russian origin
ending in accented a, will not
be declined.

Example: Бенуа́*

Those ending in unaccented a,
will be declined like feminine
nouns of the same type shown in
Figure 9.

Example: Ка́нада

5. Masculine names ending in the
letter ь in the nominative case,
will be declined like the noun
указатель in Figure 8.

Example: Гоголь

6. For cataloging purposes, names
of non-Russian origin are not
transliterated from the Russian

---

*From the French-Benois.

after returning them to the nominative case, but are shown in
the form used by the bearer of
the name, if it can be determined.
Examples are the following:

Name	Transliterated	Cataloged as
Рубенштейн	**Rubenshtein̆**	*Rubenstein*
Хук	**Khuk** ◡	*Hooke*
Торндайк	**Torndaĭk**	*Thorndyke*
Гильман	**Gil'man**	*Hillman*

An Exercise in the Translation of Names

Several sections of Russian text are
presented each with a Russian name in context (underscored). Each name is to be returned to the nominative case and transliterated as it should appear on a catalog card.

Following each section is given

1. An explanation of which declensional
pattern or guideline (pp. 62 - 67) is applicable

2. The nominative case of the name

3. The transliteration of the nominative
case of the name.

An attempt should be made to determine
the catalog form of the name in a given
section before this explanatory material is
consulted.

Russian Text: См* А. В. Исаченко, Пражское совещание по вопросам лингвистической терминологии, ИАН* СССР* т* XIX вып* 5, 1960, стр* 443-445.

Explanation: This name appears in the Russian text undeclined. As indicated in Guideline 3, it should be transliterated directly as: A. V. Isachenko.

Russian Text: Я должна прежде всего поблагодарить за огромную помощь Г. К. Смирницкую.

Explanation: The ending for this name is similar to the accusative case for the feminine name following the pattern of Нижинская (see page 65). The name in the nominative case then is Г. К. Смирницкая. The transliteration is: G. K. Smirnitskaia.

Russian Text: Я хочу также выразить свою глубокую признательность К. А. Марцишевской.

Explanation: The ending here resembles either the genitive, dative, instrumental or prepositional case for the feminine name following the pattern of Нижинская (see page 65). The name in the nominative case then is К. А. Марцишевская. The transliteration is: K. A. Martsishevskaia.

Russian Text: Автор считает своим долгом выразить глубокую признательность А. А. Реформатскому.

---

*Asterisks denote abbreviations which will be explained on pages 70 - 71.

Explanation: The ending for this name is
    similar to the dative case for the
    masculine name following the pattern of
    Нижинский (see page 64). The name in
    the nominative case then is A. A.
    Реформатский. The transliteration is:
    A. A. Reformatskiĭ·

Russian Text: Благодарность выражается
    П. С. Кузнецову.

Explanation: There are two possibilities
    here. The ending y indicates the
    dative case for masculine names which
    in the nominative case end in ин, ын,
    ов, ев, ёв. The name then would be
    П. С. Кузнецов. The transliteration
    is P. S. Kuznetsov. The y ending also
    indicates the accusative case for fem-
    inine names which in the nominative
    case end in ина, ына, ова, ева, ёва.
    The name then would be П. С. Кузнецова.
    The transliteration is P. S. Kuznetsova.
    The remainder of the sentence would
    have to be translated in order to de-
    termine the case and gender of the name.

Russian Text: Очень ценные указания были
    сделаны проф* С. Б. Бернштейном.

Explanation: As indicated in Guideline 1,
    the ending ом is the instrumental case
    for masculine names ending in a conson-
    ant in the nominative case. Returning
    it to the nominative case produces С. Б.
    Бернштейн. Guideline 6 could also be
    applied here. If this is a name of
    Russian origin, it would be translit-
    erated as S. B. Bernshtein. If the
    name is non-Russian, it would be S. B.
    Bernstein.

Russian Text: Большую помощь оказал мне
М. К. К. Уилер.

Explanation: Guideline 1 may be applied to
this name which has a consonant as its
final letter. With no case ending, the
direct transliteration from the masculine, nominative case is M. K. K.
Uiler. Guideline 6 could also be applied
here which would produce the name M. K.
K. Wheeler.

Russian Text: В этом отношении типичен
список слов, подлежащих замене,
приводимый Н. И. Жинкиным.

Explanation: In the category of names which
in the masculine, nominative case end
in ин, ын, ов, ев, ёв, the ending ым
indicates either the instrumental case
if the name were singular, or the dative
case if the name were plural. Assuming
that it is singular, the name returned
to the nominative case would be Н. И.
Жинкин. The transliteration is N. I.
Zhinkin.

Abbreviations

     Russian is no different from other
languages in that abbreviations are often
used. Sometimes, in the vocabulary of Library Science, transliteration will reveal
recognizable abbreviations if they are related to those used in the English language.
With others that are not related to anything
familiar, memorization is required. Some
abbreviations can be found in dictionaries.

     In the Russian text used in the exercise

on proper nouns (pp. 68-70), a number of
abbreviations appear which have been marked
with asterisks. In Figure 16 each abbreviation is listed in the sequence in which it
appears in the Russian text. The figure
shows the words abbreviated and what the
translations should be.

Abbreviations will be discussed again
in Chapters 9*, 10 (pg. 149) and 14 (pg. 207).

FIGURE 16

Russian Abbreviation	Abbreviation for	English Translation
см.	смотри	see
ИАН	Известие Академии Наук	Bulletin of the Academy of Sciences
СССР	Союз Советских Социалистических Республик	USSR; Union of Soviet Socialist Republics
т.	том	volume
вып.	выпуск	issue; edition
стр.	страница	page
проф.	профессор	professor

_____

*See vocabulary

Vocabulary

второ́й		Adj.	second
вы́пуск	*(m)*	N	issue, number, part; edition
изве́стие	*(n)*	N	news, information
копе́йка	*(f)*	N	kopeck
но́вый		Adj.	new
ру́сский		Adj.	Russian
состави́тель	*(m)*	N	compiler
страни́ца	*(f)*	N	page
указа́тель	*(m)*	N	index
цена́	*(f)*	N	price
число́	*(n)*	N	date, number

EXERCISE

*With the use of textbook materials, translate
these prepositions and names into English
showing the transliteration of the name in
the nominative case.*

от Волги

о Мухине

с Канадой

*For each name listed, give the case(s),
return to the nominative case (if necessary)
and transliterate:*

1. Джонсом

2. Жуковского

3. Ушинская

4. Багравой

5. Каневский

6. Семенченко

CHAPTER 5

*Predicate Adjectives**

In English, an adjective modifying a
noun either attributively

the <u>new</u> book

or predicatively

The book is <u>new</u>.

does not change in form.

But in Russian, the same adjective may
appear attributively as in

новая книга
new   book

or predicatively as in

Книга   нова .
The book is[§]*new* .

in a different form.

The predicate (short) form for the

*These adjectives generally follow the noun
 being modified; they are also known as
 short form adjectives.

§ In this type of sentence, the verb *to be*
 is implied, but only for the present tense.

75

attributive adjective новыи does not have endings which vary depending on gender, case and number. The changes that occur depend only on gender and number. The stem нов is retained for the masculine, singular as in

> Том   нов.
> *The volume is new.*

For the feminine, singular the stem нов appears with the additional letter а as in

> Школа   нова.
> *The school is new.*

For the neuter, singular the stem нов appear with the additional letter о as in

> Описание   ново.
> *The entry is new.*

And for the plural the stem нов appears with the additional letter ы as in

> Выпуски   новы.
> *The editions are new.*

When the adjective хороший appears in the predicate form it looks like this:

Masculine singular: Указатель   хорош.
                      The index is good.

Feminine singular: Цена   хороша.
                      The price is good.

Neuter singular: Известие   хорошо.
                      The news is good.

Plural: Выдержки   хороши.
                      The excerpts are good.

But for the adjective интересный (interesting), there is a slight variation which appears in the masculine, singular. If it followed the same pattern as новый and хороший it would appear as интересн. Instead, the vowel е is inserted between the two last consonants of the stem and it appears in context looking like this:

> Указатель   интересен.
> *The index is interesting.*

Predicate adjectives whose stems end in a double consonant will appear with a vowel (usually е or о) separating these consonants in the masculine singular case.

For the adjective редкий (rare), the masculine singular is редок. For the adjective трудный (difficult), the masculine singular is труден.

The feminine singular, neuter singular and plural for adjectives whose stems end in a double consonant do not vary and follow the same patterns as новый and хороший.

Adverbs

Adverbs are similar in appearance to predicate adjectives in that they also retain the stem of the attributive adjective from which they are derived and then add a vowel. For example:

Attributive adjective	Adverb
историческ│ий	историческ│и*
historical	*historically*

*The same form as the plural predicate adjective.

Attributive adjective	Adverb
груб|ый *broad*	груб|о* *broadly*
кратк|ий *short*	кратк|о* *shortly*
редк|ий *rare*	редк|о* *rarely*

The difference between adverbs and predicate adjectives is that the adverb never changes its form whereas the predicate adjective appears with endings which change depending on the gender and number of the noun being modified.

The following sentences are made up of a noun, an adverb and a predicate adjective. The attributive adjectives from which the adverb and the predicate adjective are derived are noted in parenthesis beneath each part of speech as well as the translation, in italics.

Noun	Adverb	Predicate adjective
Доклад *The report is*	исторически (исторический) *historically*	интересен. (интересный). *interesting.*
Издания *The editions are*	обычно (обычный) *usually*	редки. (редкий). *rare.*

---

*The same form as the neuter predicate adjective.

Noun   Adverb   Predicate
                                  Adjective

         Вестники   редко   кратки.
                       (редкий) (краткий).
    The reviews are   rarely   short.

Translation of Title Pages

     The librarian is often called upon to
work with title pages of various sorts.
Figures 17 and 18 are reproductions of title
pages which you are to translate completely.
These pages illustrate the use of nouns,
adjectives, proper nouns and abbreviations.
Upon completion of this exercise, translations and explanations may be consulted on
pages 82- 86.

ВОПРОСЫ ТЕОРИИ МАТЕМАТИЧЕСКИХ МАШИН

СБОРНИК ПЕРВЫЙ

Под редакцией
Ю. Я. БАЗИЛЕВСКОГО

ГОСУДАРСТВЕННОЕ ИЗДАТЕЛЬСТВО
ФИЗИКО-МАТЕМАТИЧЕСКОЙ ЛИТЕРАТУРЫ
МОСКВА 1 9 5 8

Figure 17

ГОСУДАРСТВЕННАЯ ОРДЕНА ЛЕНИНА БИБЛИОТЕКА СССР
имени В. И. ЛЕНИНА

БИБЛИОТЕКОВЕДЕНИЕ
и
БИБЛИОГРАФИЯ
ЗА РУБЕЖОМ

СБОРНИК

ВЫПУСК ДВАДЦАТЫЙ

ИЗДАТЕЛЬСТВО «КНИГА»
МОСКВА 1966

Figure 18

TRANSLATION OF TITLE PAGE IN FIGURE 17

Вопросы[1]   Теории[2]
Questions of Theory

Математических[3]
of Mathematical

Машин
Machines

Сборник[4]Первый[5]
Collection First

Под[6]редакцией[7]
Edited by

Ю. Я. Базилевского[8]
Iu.Ia. Bazilevskiĭ

Государственное[9] Издательство[10]
State   Publishing House

Физико[11]Математической[12]Литературы[13]
of Physical & Mathematical Literature

Москва[14]1958
Moscow 1958

_____

[1]вопрос *m* -а, -ов question. This noun is the
subject of the title and appears in the
nominative, plural case.

[2]теори|я *f* -и, -й theory. According to Fig-
ure 9, the   ending could be genitive,dat-
tive, prepositional, singular, or nominative,
plural cases. The genitive singular seems
to fit best in this context.

[3]Transliteration indicates that this may be
derived from *mathematics*. The ending их
(continued on next page)

is the genitive, plural case for all adjectives. The gender, case and number have been determined by the noun машин following (gentive, plural for машина).

[4] сборник *(m)* N collection.

[5] первый adj. first. Here is an exception where the attributive adjective follows the noun it modifies. This form is often seen on title pages and may be translated as - *First Collection.*

[6] Figure 11 indicates that под means *under* and requires the accusative or instrumental case. The noun following presents a further explanation.

[7] редакци|я *f* -и, -й 1. под ~ей..4. editorial board. The preposition preceding explains this noun appearing in the instrumental case. Literally, под редакцией is translated as *under the editorial board.* Since the word *of* would normally follow this idiom, any name following would appear in the genitive case (assuming it is the type of name which can be declined).

[8] The name has been returned to the nominative case. Note that the Russian initials have each been transliterated as two English letters.

[9] государственное Adj. state,national.

[10] издательство *(n)* N publishing house.

[11] This is actually an abbreviation of the adjective физический and is unchanging with regard to case. It may also be translated as *physico.*

(continued on page 84)

(continued from page 83)

[12]Since the ой ending for this adjective indicates more than one possible case, it is
best to determine the case of the noun
being modified before making a decision.

[13]литература *(f)* N literature. The ы ending
for feminine nouns indicates either the
genitive, singular, nominative plural or
accusative plural cases. The ой ending on
the adjective preceding cannot apply to
the plural case which leaves the genitive
singular as the only choice possible for
adjective and noun.

[14]Москва *(f)* N Moscow.

TRANSLATION OF TITLE PAGE IN FIGURE 18

Государственная[1]   Ордена[2] Ленина[3] Библиотека
State   of the Order of Lenin Library

СССР[4]
of the USSR

имени[5] В. И. Ленина[6]
named for V. I. Lenin

Библиотековедение[7]
Library Science

и
and

Библиография
Bibliography

за[8]Рубежом[9]
Abroad

Сборник
A collection

Выпуск Двадцатый[10]
Edition Twentieth

Издательство   "Книга"[11]
Publishing House   "Book"

---

[1]This adjective is shown in the feminine, nominative, singular case. Since the noun following is not of the feminine gender, the only other possible noun it could modify is библиотека. This separation between an adjective and the noun it is modifying sometimes occurs in the construction of Russian sentences.

(continued on next page)

[2] орден *m* -а, *pl* -а, -ов order (a decoration).
According to the dictionary entry, this noun
appears in either the genitive singular or
nominative plural case. Let us assume it
is genitive singular.

[3] The name Ленин shown in the genitive case.

[4] When initials appear in another case, there
is no ending shown. The reader must deter-
mine from the context what the case may be.
СССР appears to be in the genitive case.
The name of this library could be translated
as *USSR State Library of the Order of Lenin,*
Order of Lenin State Library of the USSR or
USSR Order of Lenin State Library.

[5] имени...*see* имя.
имя *n* имени...name *(an appellation);*

[6] The name following имени will always appear
in the genitive case. The literal translation of the phrase is *name of V. I. Lenin.*
It would seem that the library is named *for*
V. I. Lenin.

[7] библиотековедение *(n)* N library science.

[8] According to Figure 11, the meaning of this
preposition depends on the case of the noun
following. Since the noun is in the instrumental case, за means *behind, beyond, for,*
after. Final translation of the phrase depends on the meaning of the noun following.

[9] рубеж *m* -а, -ей 1. boundary, border...за
рубежом abroad.

[10] двадцатый *num ord* twentieth. Note here that
the attributive adjective follows the noun
it modifies.

[11] книга *(f)* N book. The name of the publishing house is shown here in reversed order.

Vocabulary

библиотековéдение	*(n)* N	library science
вéстник	*(m)* N	review
грýбый	Adj.	broad
доклáд	*(m)* N	report
издáние	*(n)* N	edition
издáтельство	*(n)* N	publishing house
úмени	(idiom)	named for
кнúга	*(f)* N	book
крáткий	Adj.	short
под редáкцией	(idiom)	edited by
рéдкий	Adj.	rare
сбóрник	*(m)* N	collection
хорóший	Adj.	good

EXERCISE

Translate the following title pages with the use of the dictionary:

ГОСУДАРСТВЕННАЯ ОРДЕНА ЛЕНИНА БИБЛИОТЕКА СССР
ИМЕНИ В. И. ЛЕНИНА

НАУЧНО-МЕТОДИЧЕСКИЙ ОТДЕЛ
БИБЛИОТЕКОВЕДЕНИЯ И БИБЛИОГРАФИИ

БИБЛИОТЕКОВЕДЕНИЕ И БИБЛИОГРАФИЯ

УКАЗАТЕЛЬ ЛИТЕРАТУРЫ

№ 4

Октябрь — декабрь 1965 года

ИЗДАТЕЛЬСТВО «КНИГА»
МОСКВА 1966

ВСЕСОЮЗНАЯ КНИЖНАЯ ПАЛАТА

АНГЛО-РУССКИЙ
БИБЛИОТЕЧНО-БИБЛИОГРАФИЧЕСКИЙ
СЛОВАРЬ

Составил
М. Х. САРИНГУЛЯН
Под редакцией
П. Х. КАНАНОВА и В. В. ПОПОВА

ИЗДАТЕЛЬСТВО ВСЕСОЮЗНОЙ КНИЖНОЙ ПАЛАТЫ
МОСКВА 1958

CHAPTER 6

Personal Pronouns

    Having determined that all nouns and
adjectives are declined by gender, number
and case, we find that the personal pronouns
used to refer to both animate and inanimate
nouns are also declined. Here are the pronouns shown in the nominative case first, in
order to explain proper usage in translation:

First Person

Singular   Plural

Я - I   Мы - We

Masculine or Feminine Masculine or Feminine

Second Person

Ты - You   Вы - You

Used to address male   Used to address more
or female familiarly;   than one in familiar
the plural form Вы   or polite terms.
is used to address
one politely.

(continued on next page)

(continued)

Third Person

Singular   Plural

Он*- He   Они - They

Also *it* when referring   Masculine or feminine.
to inanimate masculine   Animate or inanimate
nouns.   nouns.

Она*- She

Also *it* when referring
to inanimate feminine
nouns.

Оно*- It

When referring to
neuter nouns.

    Figure 19 shows the declension of all
the personal pronouns. In some cases they
will seem familiar since they bear a similarity to certain adjective declensions in
Figure 14. Compare, for example, the declension of the third person singular, masculine and neuter, and the third person
plural with the declension of the adjective
хороший.

---

*As an aid to memorizing these pronouns, one
 might keep in mind the fact that like он -
 many masculine nouns end in a consonant;
 like она - many feminine nouns end in а;
 like оно -many neuter nouns end in о.

Figure 19

DECLENSION OF PERSONAL PRONOUNS

First Person

	Singular	Plural
N	я	мы
G	меня	нас
D	мне	нам
A	меня	нас
I	мной	нами
P	мне	нас

Second Person

N	ты	вы
G	тебя	вас
D	тебе	вам
A	тебя	вас
I	тобой	вами
P	тебе	вас

Third Person

	Masc.	Fem.	Neut.	Plural
N	он	она	оно	они
G	(н)его*	(н)её	(н)его	(н)их
D	(н)ему	(н)ей	(н)ему	(н)им
A	(н)его	(н)её	(н)его	(н)их
I	(н)им	(н)ей	(н)им	(н)ими
P	нём	ней	нём	них

*Personal pronouns may appear with the letter
н added to them in those cases where they
are governed by a preposition. Since the
prepositional case is always governed by a
preposition, it appears in only one form.
The nominative case is never governed by a
preposition.

Verbs

The Russian verb has the distinction of appearing in two different forms:

(1) the imperfective, indicating an action that is, was, or will be going on and is not completed;

(2) the perfective, indicating an action that took place and was completed or that will be started and completed and therefore has no present tense. Each verb then has two somewhat different infinitives.

The Imperfective Verb

Most verb infinitives end in the letters ть. The following conjugations are typical for regular imperfective verbs which have ть as their final letters and also have the vowels а or я preceding the ть.

чит|ать - to read

Present Tense*   Translation

я чита ю	*I read, am reading, do read*
ты чита ешь	*You read, are reading, do read*
он чита ет	*He reads, is reading, does read*
она чита ет	*She reads, is reading, does read*
оно чита ет	*It reads§, is reading, does read*
мы чита ем	*We read, are reading, do read*
вы чита ете	*You read, are reading, do read*
они чита ют	*They read, are reading, do read*

---

*The one form of the present tense is translated as *I read, I am reading, I do read.*

§If perhaps, an inanimate neuter object reads.

измен|ять – to change

Present Tense	Translation
я изменя ю	*I change, am changing, do change*
ты изменя ешь	*You change, are changing, do change*
он изменя ет	*He changes, is changing, does change*
она изменя ет	*She changes, is changing, does change*
оно изменя ет	*It changes, is changing, does change*
мы изменя ем	*We change, are changing, do change*
вы изменя ете	*You change, are changing, do change*
они изменя ют	*They change, are changing, do change*

Note that the conjugations for the verbs shown retain the stems of the infinitives and the letters а and я before endings are added.

The dictionary entry for чит|ать

чит|ать *imperf* -аю, аешь, прочит|ать *perf*, проч|есть *perf* ....1. read ....

indicates first that this is an imperfective verb with the stem чит. Following this designation are

the beginning of the conjugational scheme аю, аешь,

two forms of the perfective (most verbs have only one),

and the definition of the verb.

Verbs which in the infinitive end with the letters итьor еть retain only the stem before the following endings:

говор|ить - to speak, talk

я говор	ю	*I speak, am speaking, do speak*
ты говор	ишь	*You speak,are speaking,do speak*
он говор	ит	*He speaks,is speaking, does speak*
она говор	ит	*She speaks,is speaking,does speak*
оно говор	ит	*It speaks, is speaking,does speak*
мы говор	им	*We speak, are speaking,do speak*
вы говор	ите	*You speak,are speaking,do speak*
они говор	ят	*They speak,are speaking,do speak*

смотр|еть - to look

я смотр	ю	*I look, am looking, do look*
ты смотр	ишь	*You look, are looking, do look*
он смотр	ит	*He looks, is looking, does look*
она смотр	ит	*She looks,is looking,does look*
оно смотр	ит	*It looks, is looking, does look*
мы смотр	им	*We look, are looking, do look*
вы смотр	ите	*You look, are looking, do look*
они смотр	ят	*They look,are looking, do look*

Verbs ending with овать

In addition to infinitives ending with the letters ать there is a class of infinitives which end in the letters овать:

редактир<u>овать</u> - to edit
публик<u>овать</u> - to publish

These verbs are conjugated like читать except that the portion of the verb retained in the conjugation is the stem preceding овать with the addition of the letter у:

редактир|овать - to edit

Present Tense   Translation

я редактир ую   *I edit, am editing, do edit*
ты редактир уешь   *You edit, are editing, do
                              edit*
он редактир ует   *He edits, is editing, does
                              edit*
она редактир ует   *She edits, is editing, does
                              edit*
оно редактир ует   *It edits, is editing, does
                              edit*
мы редактир уем   *We edit, are editing, do
                              edit*
вы редактир уете   *You edit, are editing, do
                              edit*
они редактир уют   *They edit, are editing, do
                              edit*

Since the verb ending is enough to identify which person is intended, a verb form
is sometimes shown without the personal pronoun preceding it. For example:

Говорят   о   журнале.
They are talking about the journal.

With verbs being listed in the dictionary in infinitive form, a verb form must be
returned to its infinitive before a definition can be located. The following table
shows a number of verbs with present tense
endings, the verb stems minus the endings
and the verb stems with infinitive endings:

Present Tense	Verb Stem	Infinitive
исправляет	исправл	исправлять
используют	использ	использовать
пересматриваем	пересматрив	пересматривать
множу	множ	множить

The Verb иметь - *to have*

An exception to the conjugational scheme of verbs ending with the letters еть is the verb иметь which follows the conjugation of verbs ending with the letters ать

име│ть - to have

Present Tense   Translation

я име ю	*I have, am having, do have*
ты име ешь	*You have, are having, do have*
он име ет	*He has, is having, does have*
она име ет	*She has, is having, does have*
оно име ет	*It has, is having, does have*
мы име ем	*We have, are having, do have*
вы име ете	*You have, are having, do have*
они име ют	*They have, are having, do have*

The Idiomatic Expression of - to have

Another way of expressing possession idiomatically without the use of the verb иметь is as follows:

у меня*-	*I have*
у тебя -	*You have*
у него -	*He has*
у неё -	*She has*
у него -	*It has*
у нас -	*We have*
у вас -	*You have*
у них -	*They have*

---

*This personal pronoun is governed by the preposition у (by, at) and is therefore shown in the genitive case. Literally, this phrase means - *by me*.

Using this idiom in the context of a sentence, we have

У   библиотеки   редкие книги.
By (at) the library are* rare books.
(literal translation)

The library has rare books.
(actual translation)

Irregular Verbs

There are many other verb infinitives[§] which end in the letters чь and ти and are irregularly conjugated. The following dictionary entries illustrate the irregularities in the conjugational schemes of these verbs:

мочь *imperf* могу, можешь, могут...
с|мочь *perf* be able.....

вести *imperf* веду, ведёшь,...
по|вести *perf*...1. lead....2. conduct, direct, run...

An Exercise in the Translation of Verbs

The following sentences which illustrate the use of verbs in the present tense are to be translated in the space provided.

———————

*The verb *to be*

[§]A list of all types of verbs and their conjugational schemes may be found in B. A. Lapidus and S. V. Shevtsova, *loc.cit.*, pp. 586-599.

Your work can be checked on pages 101-102 where correct translations of the sentences are given with an indication of the verb infinitive from which verb forms have been derived.

1. Он издавает доклад Сталина в Монголии.

2. Мы пересматриваем книгу с Разумовским.

3. Я иллюстрирую журнал с Бельской.

4. Мы помним книги Королева.

5. Вы переплетаете анналы Брайента.

6. Библиотекарь публикует альманах Томсона.

7. Авторы прибавляют том сборнику Жукиной.

8. Она изменяет главу Рецкера.

9. Я просматриваю книгу с Грушниковым в

Чикаго.

TRANSLATION OF EXERCISE ON PAGE 100

(издавать)
1. Он   издавает   доклад Сталина в
   He is publishing report of Stalin in

   Монголии.
   Mongolia.

(пересматривать)
2. Мы пересматриваем книгу с Разумовским.
   We are revising   book with Razumovskiĭ.

(иллюстрировать)
3. Я   иллюстрирую   журнал   с Бельской.*
   I am illustrating journal with Bel'skaĭa.

(помнить)
4. Мы помним   книги Королева.
   We remember books of Korolev.

(переплетать)
5. Вы переплетаете анналы Брайента.
   You are binding   annals of Bryant.

(публиковать)
6. Библиотекарь   публикует   альманах
   The librarian is publishing almanac

   Томсона.
   of Thomson.

(прибавлять)
7. Авторы   прибавляют том   сборнику
   The authors are adding volume to the col-

   Жукиной.*
   lection of Zhukina.

(continued on next page)

_____
*Miss or Mrs.

(изменять)
8. Она изменяет главу Рецкера.
She is revising chapter of Retsker.

(просматривать)
9. Я просматриваю книгу с Грушниковым
I am revising book with Grushnikov

в Чикаго.
in Chicago.

Vocabulary

издава́ть	Imperf.Verb	to publish
изменя́ть	Imperf.Verb	to revise
исправля́ть	Imperf.Verb	to revise
переплета́ть	Imperf.Verb	to bind
пересма́тривать	Imperf.Verb	to revise
печа́тать	Imperf.Verb	to print
просма́тривать	Imperf.Verb	to revise
публикова́ть	Imperf.Verb	to publish
редакти́ровать	Imperf.Verb	to edit
сокраща́ть	Imperf.Verb	to abridge,shorten
увели́чивать	Imperf.Verb	to enlarge
умножа́ть	Imperf.Verb	to enlarge

EXERCISE

With the use of the dictionary, find the in-
finitives and translate the verb forms shown
below:

1. показывает

2. дарит

3. измеряете

4. обслуживают

5. информируете

6. отправляем

7. характеризует

8. зависят

VOCABULARY AND TRANSLITERATION TEST

Return the transliterated word to Russian and
provide the translation.

 1. vvedenie
 2. vestnik
 3. vypusk
 4. glava
 5. gosudarstvennyi
 6. doklad
 7. zhurnal
 8. izvestie
 9. izdatel'
10. sostavitel'

CHAPTER 7

Reflexive Verbs

Library literature makes wide use of
verb forms derived from infinitives which
have attached to them the suffix ся. The
letters ся are a contraction of the reflexive pronoun себя - self, suggesting that the
subject of the verb with this additional ending may also be the receiver or object of
the action involved.

The conjugation of the reflexive verb
as it is known, is the same as that of an
ordinary verb except that the letters ся or
сь (when a vowel precedes the suffix) are
added. For example: заниматься

Я занимаюсь
ты занимаешься
он занимается
она занимается
оно занимается
мы занимаемся
вы занимаетесь
они занимаются

The procedure in defining an unknown
reflexive verb form such as

он представляется

is first to determine the infinitive in the
following manner:

105

1. Drop the suffix ся - представляет
2. Return the verb to infinitive form -
                                  представлять
3. Add the suffix ся to the infinitive
   form - представляться

The definition of this infinitive can
now be determined from the dictionary.

If one were to translate the sentence

            Книга читается

it would be found that the verb infinitive
читаться from which читается is derived, is
not listed in the dictionary. In cases
where verbs with the suffix ся are not listed in the dictionary, it is necessary to

1. Drop the suffix - читает
2. Take the dictionary definition of
   the infinitive minus the suffix -
   читать - to read
3. Add the definition of себя - self.

The sentence

            Книга читается

is then literally translated as

        The book reads self

which actually is translated in the passive
sense as

        The book is read.

Other examples of reflexive verbs being translated in the passive sense are:

Доклады   публикуются   в   журнале.
The reports publish selves in the journal.
(are published)

Вестники   печатаются   в   СССР.
The reviews print selves in the USSR.
(are printed)

To smoothly translate the reflexive
verb in these cases requires editing the
word for word dictionary definition into
American usage.

On the other hand, there are numerous
other verbs which look reflexive but are de-
fined in the dictionary like ordinary verbs.
For example:

Russian: Я справляюсь в словаре.

справл|яться *imperf* -яюсь,
-яешься,.....3. ask (about),
inquire (about).

English: *I am inquiring in (consulting)*
a dictionary.

Russian: Они учатся читать.

учи|ться *imperf* учусь, учишься,
..... learn, study...

English: *They are learning to read.*

Reflexive Verbs and the Instrumental Case

It was indicated in Chapter Three that
the object of a verb appears in either the
accusative or the dative case depending on
whether it is the direct or indirect object.

Here are some reflexive verbs which are exceptions to the rule and govern the instrumental case:

> Он становится читателем.
> *He is becoming a reader.*
>
> Она пользуется новой книгой.
> *She is using   a new book.*

Since there are no guidelines for determining which reflexive verbs govern the instrumental case, except through memorization, one should at least be aware that this construction may be present in a Russian sentence and that the translations of objects of verbs of this type follow the usual pattern even though they appear in the instrumental case.

An Exercise in Translating Reflexive Verbs

The following sentences contain a number of reflexive verbs. The sentences are to be translated in their entirety. The correct translations, and explanations are given on pages 110 - 114.

1. Библиографическое описание составляется

на языке текста книги и снабжается переводом

основных элементов описания на русский язык.

2. Бюллетень ИНИТДИ широко распространяется

в стране и рассылается более чем о 120

адресов за границу.

3. Печатные карточки Всесоюзной книжной

палаты предназначаются для использования

библиотеками в алфавитных, систематических

и предметных каталогах, а также в картотеках

библиотек.

FIGURE 20

TRANSLATION OF EXERCISE ON REFLEXIVE VERBS

1. Библиографическое описание составляется[1]
   The bibliographic   entry   is compiled

на языке[2] текста[3] книги[4] и снабжается[5]
in language of text of book and is provided

---

[1] Returning this to infinitive form produces
составляться. The dictionary only lists
составл|ять *imperf* -яю, -яешь.....compose,
compile....
which renders the literal translation of
the verb as - *compiles self*, or more
smoothly, *is compiled*.

[2] язык *m* -а, -ов....language, tongue...
Shown in the prepositional case because of
the preceding на.

[3] The meaning of this word can be guessed
from the transliteration. The dictionary
entry
текст *m* -а, -ов text.....
indicates that the ending is genitive singular.

[4] One could be misled into thinking that this
word and the word preceding are translated
as - *textbook*, except for the fact that both
текста and книги are nouns, each in the
genitive case.

[5] The same explanation holds true here as for
footnote [1] except for the definition of the
verb: снабж|ать *imperf* -аю, -аешь....
supply *(with)*, provide *(with)*...

переводом [1]   основных [2]элементов описания [3]
with translation of basic elements   of entry

на   русский   язык.
into Russian language.

2. Бюллетень   ИНИТДИ [4]   широко [5]
    The bulletin of INITDI widely

---

[1]перевод *m* -а, ов....translation....
This appears in the instrumental, singular
case.

[2]основн|ой *a* fundamental,basic, principal;..
This adjective appears in the genitive,
plural case and is followed by the noun it
modifies also in the genitive, plural case.

[3]The only case which makes sense here is the
genitive singular.

[4]These initials for Институт научной и технической документации и информации - The
Institute of Scientific and Technical Documentation and Information, are probably in
the genitive case. If the initials were
unknown, the same assumption could be made.

[5]The only dictionary entry resembling this is
широк|ий *a* -ая, ое, ие,...wide, broad...
Judging from its form and the fact that it
precedes a verb - it is an adverb.

FIGURE 20 (continued)

распространяется[1]в   стране   и рассылается[2]
is circulated   country and   is sent

более[3]чем   в   120   адресов[4] за границу[5]
more   than   to 120 addresses   abroad.

---

[1]The infinitive for this verb form is listed
in the dictionary:
распростран|яться *imperf* -яется,..spread...
But a smoother translation is rendered by
using the definition in the dictionary entry
for the non-reflexive infinitive:
распростран|ять *imperf* -яю, -яешь,..circu-
late.....(in the passive sense).

[2]The passive sense is again applied to this
dictionary entry
рассыл|ать *imperf* -аю, -аешь,..send...

[3]более *adv used to form comp;* не   чем not
more than...

[4]The genitive, plural ending for this noun
is explained in Chapter 14.

[5]This idiom is shown under the dictionary
entry for
границ|а *f* -ы,   ..поехать за ~y go abroad..

3. Печатные[1] карточки[2] Всесоюзной[3]
   The printed cards of the All-Union

книжной[4] палаты[5]предназначаются[6]для
book Chamber are intended for

использования[7]библиотеками в алфавитных[8]
use by libraries in alphabetic

---

[1]печатный *Adj*. printed

[2]карточ|ка *f* -ки, -ек card...

[3]всесоюзный *a* All-Union....

[4]книжный *a* ..book...
The adjective form of the noun книга is
aberrant as is evident in the change of the
letter г to ж.

[5]палат|а *f* -ы, ~ ..chamber...
The official name of this organization is
The All-Union Book Chamber.

[6]The passive sense is applied to the dictionary definition for the infinitive
предназнач|ать *imperf* -аю, -аешь,..intend

[7]This is apparently a noun in the genitive
case, governed by the preposition для preceding it. The only dictionary entry resembling it is the verb infinitive
использ|овать ..*imperf* -ую, -уешь,..use

[8]алфавитный каталог *(m)* Adj. N-alphabetical
                                        catalog.

FIGURE 20 (continued)

систематических¹ и предметных²каталогах³ а
    classified   and subject   catalogs and

также⁴ в картотеках⁵ библиотек.
also in card files of libraries.

---

¹систематический каталог *(m)* Adj. N classified catalog.
Although the dictionary entry is
систематическ|ий *a* -ая, -ое,-ие systematic..
the preferred definition, when referring to
a catalog is *classified*.

²предметный Adj. subject

³каталог *m* -а, -ов catalog
This noun and the three adjectives preceding
it are all in the prepositional, plural case
governed by the в preceding the entire
phrase.

⁴также *adv* also...

⁵картотек|а *(f)* N card file

Vocabulary

алфави́тный		Adj.	alphabetical
катало́г	*(m)*	N	catalog
всесою́зный		Adj.	all-union, national, federal
картоте́ка	*(f)*	N	card file
ка́рточка	*(f)*	N	card
перево́д	*(m)*	N	translation
печа́тный		Adj.	printed
предме́тный		Adj.	subject
системати́ческий		Adj.	classified
катало́г	*(m)*	N	catalog

EXERCISE

Translate the following sentences with the use of the dictionary:

1. Описание приводится в картотеке.

2. Карточки получаются в библиотеке.

3. Автор характеризуется в вестнике.

4. Вы пользуетесь старым словарём?

5. Книги описываются в бюллетене.

CHAPTER 8

The Imperfective Future Tense

The imperfective future tense of verbs is formed by combining the future tense of the verb быть* - *to be*, with the imperfective verb infinitive. Before proceeding then, it is necessary to consider the conjugation of the verb быть in the future tense, which is somewhat irregular:

я	буду	*I shall be*
ты	будешь	*you will be*
он	будет	*he will be*
она	будет	*she will be*
оно	будет	*it will be*
мы	будем	*we shall be*
вы	будете	*you will be*
они	будут	*they will be*

The imperfective future of the verb читать is:

я буду читать	*I shall read, be reading*
ты будешь читать	*you will read, be reading*
он будет читать	*he will read, be reading*
она будет читать	*she will read, be reading*
оно будет читать	*it will read, be reading*
мы будем читать	*we shall read, be reading*
вы будете читать	*you will read, be reading*
они будут читать	*they will read, be reading*

---

*This verb was first introduced in Chapter 5 (pg. 75) as sometimes being implied in sentences- only in the present tense.

The Perfective Verb (Perfective Future Tense)

   Imperfective and perfective verbs were
first introduced in Chapter 6. The perfective verb was described as one in which an
action is indicated as having taken place
and been completed, or one that would be
started and completed, and therefore had no
present tense. Although the perfective verb
differs in appearance from the imperfective,
it is conjugated like the imperfective present but is translated in the future tense:

прочитать - to read

я	прочитаю	*I shall read*
ты	прочитаешь	*you will read*
он	прочитает	*he will read*
она	прочитает	*she will read*
оно	прочитает	*it will read*
мы	прочитаем	*we shall read*
вы	прочитаете	*you will read*
они	прочитают	*they will read*

   Since the conjugation of the perfective
verb resembles that of the imperfective in
the present tense, in order to render an
accurate translation it is necessary to determine which one we are dealing with. In
the case of the imperfective verb, the dictionary entry specifies *imperf*. The typical
entry for a perfective verb like прочитать
is:

прочитать *see* читать

   The reader is directed to the entry*for

---

*This verb is unusual in that it has two
 forms for the perfective.

чит|ать *imperf* -аю, -аешь, прочит|ать
perf, проч|есть *perf* -ту, -тёшь,....

where the conjugational pattern is indicated
for the perfective as well as the imperfective
verb.

There are many other verbs like прочитать which may be recognized as perfective
because they are formed by the addition of a
prefix to the imperfective forms. Examples
of these verbs are:

Imperfective	Perfective	
писать	написать	*to write*
комплектовать	укомплектовать	*to acquire*
редактировать	отредактировать	*to edit*
публиковать	опубликовать	*to publish*

Another group of perfective verbs are
similar to the imperfective except for a
change in the suffix:

Imperfective	Perfective	
изменять	изменить	*to revise*
составлять	составить	*to compile*

Another type of perfective verb is formed by eliminating a syllable from the imperfective form:

Imperfective	Perfective	
издавать	издать	*to publish*
описывать	описать	*to describe*

And still another group of perfective verbs takes a completely different form from its perfective:

Imperfective   Perfective

говорить   сказать   *to speak*
брать   взять   *to take*

Past Passive Participles

The past passive participle may also be called a verbal adjective in the sense that it is a part of speech which is derived from a verb (usually perfective) and performs the function of an adjective in a sentence.

The masculine nominative ending аннЫй may be traced to infinitives ending in ать:

Past Passive Participle Infinitive

отредактиров<u>анный</u>   отредактиров<u>ать</u>
из<u>данный</u>   из<u>дать</u>
напечат<u>анный</u>   напечат<u>ать</u>

The masculine nominative ending еннЫй is traced to infinitives ending in ить and еть:

Past Passive Participle Infinitive

измен<u>енный</u>   измен<u>ить</u>
пересмотр<u>енный</u>   пересмотр<u>еть</u>

And the ending тЫй is derived from some verbs ending in ять:

Past Passive Participle   Infinitive

принятый   принять
взятый   взять

Properly declined in the context of a sentence, the past passive participle looks like this:

Газета,   <u>прочитанная</u>   студентом
The newspaper, (which was) read by the student

Обозрение   книги,   <u>опубликованной</u>
The review of the book, (which was) published

In cases where the conjugation of a perfective verb is somewhat irregular, as in

составить - *to compile*

я составлю
ты составишь
он, она, оно составит
мы составим
вы составите
они составят

the past passive participle retains the irregularity shown in the first person singular and becomes составленный. To return to the infinitive, then, it would be necessary to replace ленный with ить.

There are other adjectives with similar endings which are not necessarily past passive participles. They can be found in the dictionary, whereas the past passive participle cannot. Some of these are:

иностра<u>нны</u>й - *foreign*
карма<u>нны</u>й*- *pocket*

Shortened Form of the Past Passive Participle

Like the predicate adjective, the endings for the shortened form of the past passive participle depend only on number and gender of the subjects to which they refer. In the case of the past passive participle составленный (derived from составить), the shortened forms are:

Masculine singular   составлен

Feminine singular   составлен<u>а</u>

Neuter singular   составлен<u>о</u>

Plural   составлен<u>ы</u>

In the context of a sentence, the short-ened form looks like this:

Пособие <u>переплётено</u>.
The textbook is bound.

Словарь   <u>исчерпан</u>.
The dictionary is out of print.

The following sentence makes use of both forms of the past passive participle:

<u>Избранные</u> произведения, <u>измененные</u>
The selected   works,   revised

на   базе   доклада,   <u>напечатаны</u>
on the basis of the report, are printed

---

*As in карманный словарь - *pocket dictionary*.

в   сборнике.
in the collection.

And in the future tense:

Названия   докладов,   прочитанных на
The titles of the reports,   read   at

конференции   <u>будут</u> <u>составлены</u>.
the conference will be   compiled.

*An Exercise in Translating the Future Imper-
    fective and the Past Passive Participle*

The following paragraph* is to be translated completely. A translation and explanation is provided on pages 125-127.

Сводный каталог иностранных периодических

изданий, представленных в фондах 120

публичных, университетских, научных и

специальных библиотек ФРГ, а также Западного

Берлина. Когда работа будет завершена, она

---

*Excerpted from *Unesco Bulletin for Libraries*,
  Vol. XIV, No. 5, September-October 1960,
  Page 241.

(continued from page 123)

составит 3 тома, общим объёмом 2800 страниц;

один из них будет содержать вспомогательные

указатели. Ежегодно будет издаваться по

шесть частей - каждая объёмом 120 страниц.

Работа в целом будет содержать около 46000

названий с полными библиографическими

описаниями и 28000 отсылок.

TRANSLATION OF EXERCISE ON PAGES 123 - 124

Сводный[1] каталог иностранных[2] периодических
Union   catalog of foreign   periodic

изданий, представленных[3] в фондах[4] 120
editions,   presented   in holdings of 120

публичных, университетских, научных   и
public,   university,   research and

специальных библиотек ФРГ,[5]   а также
special   libraries of FRG, as well as

Западного Берлина. Когда работа будет
of West Berlin.   When the work will be

---

[1] сводный каталог *(m)* Adj. N-union catalog

[2] иностранный *Adj.* foreign
As indicated on page 122, this is an ordinary adjective shown in the plural genitive
case modifying the noun изданий which
follows.

[3] The past passive participle of представить:
представл|ять ....представ|ить *perf* -лю,
-ишь,....1...present...
with a genitive plural ending in agreement
with the noun изданний preceding.

[4] фонд *(m)* N stock, holding

[5] These initials represent *The Federal Republic of Germany.*

(continued from page 125)

завершена,[6] она составит 3 тома,[7]
completed, it will consist of 3 volumes,

    общим   объёмом   2800 страниц;один из
with total volume of 2800 pages; one of

  них будет содержать вспомогательные
them will   contain   auxiliary

указатели. Ежегодно[8] будет   издаваться
indexes.   Annually (it) will be published

по шесть частей - каждая объёмом   120
in six   parts - each with a volume of 120

страниц. Работа   в целом[9] будет содержать
pages. The work as a whole will   contain

   около   46000 названий с полными
approximately 46000 titles with complete

---

[6]
The future of the verb быть and the short
form of the past passive participle for the
verb завершить:
заверш|ать....заверш|ить *perf* -у, -ишь,...
complete, conclude.

[7]
Shown in the genitive singular case. This
irregularity is explained in Chapter 14,
page 201.

[8]
Related to ежегодник *(m)* N annual, yearbook

[9]
цел|ый II *as a noun* цел|ое *n* -ого (the)
whole;
Even though this adjective is used idiomatically as a noun, it is declined like an
adjective.

библиографическими   описаниями   и   28000
   bibliographic   descriptions and 28000

отсылок.[1]
references.

---

[1]
отсылка *(f)* N reference
Note the irregular ending of this genitive
plural form. The insertion of the о between
the л and the к makes it easier to pronounce.

Vocabulary

ББК			Библиотечно-Библио-графическая Класс-ификация[1]
ежегóдник	*(m)*	N	annual, yearbook
и́збранные произведéния	*(Plu.)*	Adj. N	selected works
иностра́нный		Adj.	foreign
исчéрпывать исчéрпать	Imperf.verb Perf.verb		to exhaust
карма́нный слова́рь	*(m)*	Adj. N	pocket dictionary
МГУ			Московский Государст-венный Университет[2]
назва́ние	*(n)*	N	title
отсы́лка	*(f)*	N	reference
пóлный		Adj.	complete, full
посóбие	*(n)*	N	textbook
прибавлéние	*(n)*	N	appendix, supplement
свóдный катало́г	*(m)*	Adj. N	union catalog
фóнд	*(m)*	N	stock, holdings

---

[1] Library-Bibliographic Classification
[2] Moscow State University

EXERCISE

Translate the following with the use of the dictionary:

I.   Д. А. Тарасюк и О. Б. Фомин
                     (Научная библиотека имени А.
                     М. Горького Московского
                     государственного университета
                     имени М. В. Ломоносова)

    Научная библиотека имени А. М. Горького
МГУ более десяти лет занимается организацией
систематического каталога по схеме, основанной
на ранних вариантах ББК.

II.
    Газета будет микрофильмироваться на 35
мм плёнке в соответствии с американскими
стандартами, принятыми для микрофильмирования.

CHAPTER 9

The Past Tense

The past tense for regular verbs, imperfective and perfective, takes the following form:

Past Tense

читать - прочитать

1st, 2nd, 3rd person singular
Masculine

я, ты, он читал,   *I, you, he read, was*
  прочита<u>л</u>   *(were) reading*

1st, 2nd, 3rd person singular
Feminine

я, ты, она чита<u>ла</u>,   *I, you, she read,*
  прочита<u>ла</u>   *(were) reading*

Neuter

оно читало,   *it read, was reading*
  прочитало

1st, 2nd, 3rd person plural

мы, вы, они читали,   *we, you, they read,*
  прочитали   *(were) reading*

Like the short forms of adjectives and

past passive participles, the endings beyond the letter л agree with the subject in gender and number.

To determine the infinitive of a verb from the past tense then, it is necessary to drop the endings л, ла, ло, ли and add the infinitive ending ть. For example:

Past Tense	Infinitive
составля<u>ло</u>	составля<u>ть</u>
печата<u>ла</u>	печата<u>ть</u>
издава<u>л</u>	издава<u>ть</u>
изда<u>ли</u>	изда<u>ть</u>

Some examples of the past tense shown in sentence construction are:

Мы прочитали   о   издателе.
We   read   about the publisher.

Издатель   печатал   обозрения ежедневно.
The publisher printed the reviews   daily.

Past Tense of the Verb быть

It was explained in Chapter 7 that the present tense of the commonly used verb быть is irregular. The following sentences illustrate the *past* tense which is completely regular.

(a) Книга   была взята   читателем.
    The book was taken by the reader.

(b)   Выпуски были изданы.
    The issues were published.

(c) Он был автором.
He was an author.

Note the irregularity in (c). The object following the past tense of выть appears in the instrumental case.

Past Tense of Reflexive Verbs

In Chapter 7 the reflexive verb was conjugated in the present tense. One example of its use in a sentence is:

Выпуски   издаются.
The issues are published.

The following sentence

Выпуски   издались.
The issues were published.

illustrates the same reflexive verb in the past tense (the ending ся is changed to сь since as explained in Chapter 7, it follows a vowel, in this case и). It should be noted that the Russian sentence in this illustration and the sentence shown in (b) in the section above, although using different parts of speech, are translated in the same way.

To determine the infinitive for the reflexive past tense, the following process is applied:

                        Reflexive past издались
            Drop the reflexive ending издали
            Drop the past tense ending изда
Add the reflexive infinitive ending издаться

In the case of the imperfective reflexive verb

Газета   издавалась ежегодно.
The newspaper was published annually.

the same procedure would be followed:

Reflexive past издавалась
Drop the reflexive ending издавала
Drop the past tense ending издава
Add reflexive infinitive ending издава<u>ться</u>

An Exercise in Translating the Past Tense

The following paragraphs are to be translated completely. Translations and explanations are provided on pages 136-139.

1. По совету библиотекаря я начала с

произведений М. Горького и читала их

параллельно с переводами на азербайджанский

язык. Библиотекарь пообещала подготовить

для меня рекомендательный список литературы.

2. Участие Библиотеки в международном

библиотечном сотрудничестве всемерно

развивалось и укреплялось. Библиотека

осуществляла международный книгообмен с

3058 организациями 90 стран мира.

3. Сообщение И. В. Трутневой активно

обсуждалось. Члены Бюро одобрили работу и

высказали ряд замечаний и предложений.

TRANSLATION OF EXERCISE ON PAGES 134 - 135

1. По   совету[1]   библиотекаря   я начала[2]
On the advice of the librarian I began

с   произведений М. Горького   и   читала
from the works   of M. Gor'kii and   read

их[3] параллельно[4]   с   переводами   на
them in parallel with translations in

азербайджанский   язык.[5]   Библиотекарь
Azerbaijan   language. The librarian

---

[1]
совет *m* -а, -ов 1. advice, counsel

[2]
The feminine past tense for the perfective
verb
начать *see* начинать
начин|ать *imperf* ...нач|ать *perf* -ну, -нёшь,
p начал, -ала, начало, начали,....begin,
start, commence

[3]
их *I gen & acc of* они

[4]
This is the adverbial form of the adjective
параллельн|ый *a* ....parallel

[5]
язык *(m)* N language

пообещала[1] подготовить для меня[2] рекоменд-
promised to prepare for me a recommend-

ательный список[3] литературы.
ed   list of literature.

   2.   Участие[4]   библиотеки в
     Participation of the library in

международном библиотечном сотрудничестве[5]
international   library   collaboration

       всемерно[6]   развивалось[7] и
in every possible way was developed and

---

[1] This appears to be the feminine past tense
of a verb which is not listed in the dictionary. However, by dropping the prefix
по, we have the related verb
обещ|ать *perf & imperf* -аю,-аешь   promise

[2] меня *gen & acc of* я

[3] список *(m)* N list

[4] участи|е *n* -я 1. part, participation

[5] From the adjectives preceding, this word
seems to be a noun which does not appear
in the dictionary. The word which has the
same root is the verb
сотруднич|ать *imperf*....collaborate

[6] всемерно *adv* in every possible way

[7] This verb appears in the dictionary as an
ordinary verb as well as a reflexive one
with about the same meaning:
развив|ать *imperf*.. -аю, -аешь...develop

(continued from page 137)

укреплялось.[1]   Библиотека осуществляла[2]
strengthened.   *The library carried out*

международный книгообмен[3] с   3058
international exchange with 3058

организациями   90   стран   мира.[4]
organizations of 90 countries of the world.

   3. Сообщение[5] И. В. Трутневой   активно[6]
      The report of I. V. Trutneva actively

----

[1] The passive sense is applied to the
  translation of the verb
  укрепл|ять *imperf* .... strengthen

[2] осуществл|ять *imperf* .... carry out

[3] книгообмен *(m)* N exchange

[4] The dictionary lists two meanings:
  мир *m* -а (-у), ... world, universe
  мир *m* -а peace

[5] сообщени|е *(n)* N proceedings, report

[6] This is the adverbial form of the adjective
  активн|ый *a* ... active

обсуждалось.[1]   Члены   Бюро[2]
was discussed.   The members of the Bureau

одобрили[3] работу и высказали[4] ряд[5]
endorsed the work and expressed a number

замечаний[6]   и предложений.[7]
of observations and suggestions.

---

[1]
Dropping the reflexive past tense ending
and adding the infinitive ending produces
the verb
обсужд|ать *imperf* -аю, -аешь.....
discuss; consider

[2]
Transliteration is enough here to provide
the meaning. Note that this is a proper
noun ending in the letter o and therefore,
is not declined although it is in the
genitive case.

[3]
The plural past tense for the perfective
verb
одобрить *see* одобрять
одобр|ять *imperf* ... одобр|ить *perf*...
p ‑ил....approve, endorse

[4]
The plural past tense for the perfective
verb
высказать *see* высказывать
высказыв|ать *imperf* ....выска|зать
... p ‑зал... tell, state; express

[5]
ряд *m* ‑а (‑у)....3. number (of)

[6]
замечани|е *n* ‑я, ‑и 1. remark, observation

[7]
предложени|е *n* ‑я, ‑й 2.....suggestion

Vocabulary

книгообмён	*(m)*	N	exchange
сообщёние	*(n)*	N	proceedings,report
спйсок	*(m)*	N	list
язьк	*(m)*	N	language

Abbreviation	*Abbreviated for*	*Translation*
г	год	year
э	экземпляр	copy
ж	журнал	periodical
и.т.д.	и так далее	etcetera
л	лист	leaf
М	Москва	Moscow
пер.	переплёт перевод	binding translation
р.	рубль	ruble

EXERCISE

Translate the following with the use of the dictionary:

1. Классификация наук была философским проблемом.

2. Печатная карточка рассылалась 86 библиотекам.

3. Систематическая картотека и библиотечная картотека увеличились.

4. В феврале 1925 года В. И. Невский был назначен директором Государственной библиотеки СССР имени В. И. Ленина и осуществил её реорганизацию.

5. Проблемы организации каталогов были подняты.

CHAPTER 10

The Present Active Participle

Another participle used more commonly in literary material than in conversation, is the present active participle. This participle is derived from the third person plural of the present tense of an imperfective verb:

Present Active Participle	Derived from	Infinitive
читающий	читают	читать
составляющий	составляют	составлять
говорящий	говорят	говорить
редактирующий	редактируют	редактировать

As shown above, the last letter of the third person plural ending is replaced with the letter щ, which is then followed by appropriate adjective endings (corresponding to the noun being modified).

The participle may precede the noun:

читающая машина
reading   machine

or follow it:

машина, читающая --
machine, reading (which reads)__

An example of the present active participle in the context of a sentence is:

Каталог   необходим библиотекам,
The catalog is necessary to libraries,

собирающим и организующим фонды
collecting and organizing   stocks

литературы.
of literature.

The present active participles shown above, собирающим and организующим, are both in the dative plural case modifying the noun библиотекам. To determine the infinitives for these participles, the following procedure is used:

Present active participles:	собирающим организующим
Drop participle ending:	собираю организую
Drop third person plural ending remaining:	собир организ
Add infinitive ending:	собирать организовать

Word Formation

In order to understand the functions of words in a Russian sentence and thus to translate them, it has been necessary to become familiar with declensional and conjugational endings of words. Some knowledge of how certain parts of speech are formed would now help in furthering this understanding.

It has already been explained that
there are some typical endings which indicate that certain words are verb infinitives.
Here are some verb infinitives converted
into nouns by exchanging the infinitive ending for the endings ение or ание:

Verb Infinitive	Noun
дополнять *to add*	дополнение *addition*
издать *to publish*	издание *publication*
продолжать *to continue*	продолжение *continuation*
назвать *to name*	название *title*
составлять *to compile*	составление *compilation*

Note that in each case, the English
word ends with the spelling *tion*. The following Russian nouns have in common the ending ция - also translated into *tion* in English:

классификация
classification

компиляция
compilation

информация
information

The endings тель and чик (or ик) denote
nouns which usually imply an occupation of

some sort. The following nouns are also related to verb infinitives:

Noun	Verb Infinitive
издатель *publisher*	издать *to publish*
писатель *author*	писать *to write*
составитель *compiler*	составить *to compile*
читатель *reader*	читать *to read*
переводчик *translator*	переводить *to translate*
переплётчик *binder*	переплетать *to bind*
сотрудник *co-worker*	сотрудничать *to collaborate*

A number of words are formed by combining a preposition, as a prefix with another
complete word:

вышесказанный
aforesaid

выше - *above*
сказанный - *said*

безынтересный*
uninteresting

без-*without*
интересный - *interesting*

*и may change to ы when following з.

бесплатный*
gratis

без - *without*
платный - *paid*

международный
international

между - *between*
народный - *national*

    Occasionally one comes across a seem-
ingly complex word which cannot be found in
the dictionary. By analyzing the word, it
can often be broken down into two parts each
of which *can* be found in the dictionary (perhaps with a slight variation). For example:

Великобритания
Great Britain

великий - *great*
Британия - *Britain*

многотомный
voluminous

много - *many*
том   - *volume*

средневековый
medieval

средний - *middle*
век - *age*

    A number of compound words are formed

*з may change to с when preceded by п.

by combining only the initial syllables of
two or more words into one **complete** word.
For example:

Комсомол
Young Communist League

The syllable Ком is the first syllable
of the Russian word

Коммунистический
Communist

Co is the first syllable of the word

Союз
Union

Мол is the first syllable of the word

Молодёжи
of Youth

Another example is the word

Госиздат
State Publishing House

The first syllable is from the word

Государственный
State

And the last syllable is from the word

издательство
publishing house

Another type of compound word is formed by combining the initial syllable of one

word with another whole word. For example:

редколлегия
editorial board

Ред is derived from the word

редакционная
editorial

and коллегия is the word for *board*.

There are also compounds formed from the initial letters of two or more words:

ТАСС

T̲елеграфное а̲генство   С̲оветского С̲оюза.
T̲elegraph a̲gency of̲ the S̲oviet U̲nion.

Another example is

ВИНИТИ

В̲сесоюзный И̲нститут   Н̲аучной   и̲
A̲ll-Union I̲nstitute of S̲cientific an̲d

T̲ехнической И̲нформации.
T̲echnical I̲nformation.

Word Order

The word order of a Russian sentence is sometimes confusing. The subject, for ex- ample, may appear at the end of a sentence:

В   республике организированы библиотеки.
In the republic are organized libraries.

or

Libraries in the republic are organized.

В журнале ежегодно публикуются обозрения.
In journal annually are published reviews.

or

Reviews are published annually in the journal.

Or an entire phrase may appear misplaced:

Доклад "Проблемы Комплектования и
The report "Problems of Acquisition and

Обмена Иностранной Литературы" сделал
of Exchange of Foreign Literature" made

Директор Государственной Библиотеки в
the director of the State   Library   in

Праге Я. Кунц.
Prague IA͡. Kunt͡s.

By placing the subject, verb and object of the sentence in proper order, the sentence would better be translated as:

IA͡. Kunt͡s, Director of the State Library of Prague, made the report "Problems of Acquisition and Exchange of Foreign Literature".

Here is another example of confusing word order:

Источником комплектования фондов
The source of acquisition of holdings

зарубежной литературой является между-
of foreign literature   is   inter-

народный книгообмен.
national   exchange.

    The subject of the sentence above is -
international exchange. The verb является
requires its object to be in the instrumental case - источником. The sentence can now
be translated less awkwardly as:

    *International exchange is the source of
acquisition of holdings of foreign literature.*

    Accordingly, it is of major importance,
when analyzing and translating a complex
Russian sentence, to associate the adjective
and verb with the correct noun, depending on
case endings which must agree. It is also
necessary to be aware of irregularities,
e. g. verbs which require their objects in
particular cases; prepositions which require
special cases; the use of idioms.

*An Exercise in Translating Present Active
    Participles and Complex Sentences*

    The following sentences are to be
translated completely. Translations and explanations are provided on pages 153-155.

    1. Специалистам предоставлялись все виды

обслуживания, отвечающие научному характеру

библиотеки.

2. Интересна организация работы между-

библиотечного центра Англии — Национальной

библиотеки абонемента научной и технической

литературы, приобретающей все издания,

недоступные другим библиотекам.

I. Специалистам[1] предоставлялись[2] все[3]
    To specialists   were given   all

виды[4] обслуживания,   отвечающие[5]
sorts of service,   corresponding

    научному   характеру[6] библиотеки.
to the scientific   nature of the library.

---

[1] This noun, an indirect object in the dative
plural case, awkwardly appears first.

[2] In reversed word order, this plural verb
precedes the noun it refers to - виды.
The translation given is for the reflexive
past tense.

[3] все *pron pl..see* весь.
весь 1 *pron def m*...вся *f*, всё *n*, все
all...

[4] вид *m* -а..*pl* -ы, -ов 1. kind, sort

[5] отвеч|ать *imperf* -аю, -аешь 1. answer..
This is an example of the present active
participle in the nominative plural case,
relating to the subject of the sentence -
виды. In the context of a sentence, it is
suggested that this participle might best
be translated as - *corresponding* - instead
of - *answering*.

[6] характер *m* -а, -ов...2. nature...

(continued from page 153)

The following revision of sentence 1 on page 153 renders it more readable:

All sorts of service, corresponding to the scientific nature of the library, were given to specialists.

    2.   Интересна[1]   организация
    Is interesting the organization

работы междубиблиотечного[2]центра
of work of the interlibrary center

  Англии - Национальной библиотеки -
of England - The national library

абонемента[3] научной   и   технической
    loan   of science and technological

---

[1] This short form for the adjective интересная appears in reverse order at the beginning of the sentence. It agrees in number and gender with the noun организация.

[2] An example of a compound word made up of two complete words - между - *between*, and библиотечного - *library* (genitive, singular).

[3] абонемент *(m)* N subscription, loan

литературы[1] приобретающей[2] все издания
literature, which acquires all editions

недоступные[3] другим библиотекам.
inaccessible to other libraries.

The following revision of sentence 2
on pages 154-155 renders it more readable:

The organization of work of the inter-
library center of England - The National
Lending Library for Science and Technology,
which acquires all editions inaccessible
to other libraries, is interesting.

---

[1] This library is officially known as The
National Lending Library for Science and
Technology.

[2] приобрет|ать *imperf* -аю, -аешь,...acquire.
This is an example of the present active
participle in the feminine, genitive singular case in agreement with Национальной
библиотеки (on the previous page).

[3] This adjective appears in the accusative
plural case in agreement with the noun preceding - издания.

Vocabulary

абонемéнт	*(m)*	N	loan, subscription
библиотéчное дéло	*(n)*	Adj. N	library science
год	*(m)*	N	year
годовóй		Adj.	annual
двухлéтний		Adj.	biennial
двухмéсячный		Adj.	bimonthly
дополнéние	*(n)*	N	addition, supplement
ежегóдник	*(m)*	N	annual, yearbook
ежегóдный		Adj.	yearly
ежеднéвный		Adj.	daily
ежеквартáлник	*(m)*	N	quarterly
ежемéсячный		Adj.	monthly
еженедéлный		Adj.	weekly
зарубéжный		Adj.	foreign
между-библиотéчный		Adj.	interlibrary
переводúть перевестú	Imperf.Verb Perf.Verb		to translate
перевóдчик	*(m)*	N	translator
писáтель	*(m)*	N	author

полугодовный		Adj.	half yearly
полутóм	(m)	N	half volume
продолжéние	(n)	N	continuation
собрáние	(n)	N	collection
составлéние	(n)	N	compilation
сотрýдник	(m)	N	co-worker

EXERCISE

Translate the following with the use of the dictionary:

1. В системе библиотек, обслуживающих научных работников, значительное место занимают библиотеки институтов и научно-исследовательских учреждений.

2. Включаются книги и журнальные статьи, отражающие общее состояние и отдельные проблемы библиотечного дела и библиографии за рубежом.

3. Печатающий телеграф с успехом применяется для быстрых международных межбиблиотечных связей.

CHAPTER II

Comparison of Adjectives

This section will cover three different degrees of comparison of adjectives - the positive, the comparative and the superlative.

The adjective as dealt with in all previous chapters, is the positive degree, e.g.

интересный	*interesting*
краткий	*short*
редкий	*rare*

The Comparative Degree

There are two forms for the comparative degree of adjectives. The less common form, the simple comparative, appears with the suffix ее added to the stem of the positive adjective. It is not declined:

Simple Comparative	Positive
новее *newer*	новый *new*
быстрее *quicker*	быстрый *quick*

This form is used only predicatively.
For example:

> Эта книга   интереснее.
> *This book is more interesting.*

Here are some other forms of the simple
comparative:

Simple Comparative	Positive
кратче *shorter*	краткий *short*
лучше *better*	хороший *good*
шире *wider*	широкий *wide*
реже *more rare*	редкий *rare*

Note that in some cases there is no
similarity between the comparative and the
positive degree.

Many forms of the simple comparative
can be found in the dictionary. The meanings of others can be guessed because there
is some similarity in the stems of the two
forms: кратче - краткий.

Here are two examples of sentences
dealing with the simple comparative. Note
that although the translations are alike,
the sentences are somewhat different in construction:

1. Первый   учебник   интереснее
   The first textbook is more interesting

чем   второй   учебник.
than the second textbook.

2. Первый   учебник   интереснее
   The first textbook is more interesting

   второго   учебника.
than the second textbook.

Sentence (1) is translated word for word.

In sentence (2) the word чем has been omitted and the comparative degree of the adjective, интереснее, is followed by the genitive case of the object being compared - второго учебника. This formation results in the same translation as sentence (1).

The Compound Comparative

The compound comparative degree of adjectives, the most common form of the comparative degree, combines the adverb более *(more)* or менее *(less)* with the positive degree of the adjective:

более редкая книга
the more rare book

менее интересная глава
the less interesting chapter

In these cases более and менее as adverbs, are undeclined, whereas the adjectives will be declined in agreement with the nouns being modified.

The Superlative Degree

The superlative degree of adjectives
falls into two classes - the simple superlative and the compound superlative.

The simple superlative, at first appearance, may be confused with the present
active participle discussed in Chapter 10,
pages 143-144. Whereas the present active
participle in the nominative singular case
looks like this:

читающий
читающая
читающее

the simple superlative in the nominative
singular case is as follows:

интереснейший
интереснейшая
интереснейшее

The simple superlative degree of the
adjective retains the stem интересн of the
positive degree from which it is derived -
in this case интересный, and takes on the
suffix ейш or айш followed by appropriate
adjective endings depending on the noun being modified. For example:

Simple Superlative   Positive

редчайший*том   редкий

_____
*The last letter of some adjective stems may
 change from к to ч when forming the superlative.

Simple Superlative	Positive
быстрейшая машина	быстрый
кратчайшее введение	краткий

The Compound Superlative

The compound superlative degree of adjectives is made up of the auxiliary adjective самый and the positive adjective, both declined in agreement with the noun being modified:

самый   интересный выпуск
the (a) most interesting issue

самая   интересная   библиография
the (a) most interesting bibliography

самое   интересное   составление
the (a) most interesting compilation

Another form of the compound superlative is:

наиболее   интересный   том
the (a) most interesting volume

In this form, the auxiliary наиболее remains constant and only интересный is declined.

Here are some examples of the superlative in the context of a sentence:

В этом библиотеке   редчайшие книги.
In this library   are the rarest books.

2. Собрание   славянских книг
The collection of Slavic books

является найболее обширным в   УССР.
is   the most extensive in the USSR.

3. Они   были самыми редкими книгами
They were   the rarest   books
в Москве.
in Moscow.

The Present Passive Participle

In Chapters 9 and 10, two types of
participles, the past passive and the present active, used mainly in literary Russian,
were discussed. Another participle of this
type is the present passive formed from the
first person plural of the present tense of
imperfective verbs:

Present Passive Participle	Derived from	Infinitive
читаемый	читаем	читать
переводимый	переводим	переводить
иллюстрируемый	иллюстрируем	иллюстрир-овать

As shown above, the first person plural
form is retained in its entirety and appropriate adjective endings are added depending on the noun being modified.

Here are some examples of the present
passive participle translated in the context
of a sentence:

1.   Включаемая   в указатель
(Being) included in the index

литература   освещает   теорию
the literature throws light on the theory

и   практику библиотечной и библио-
and practise   of library   and biblio-

графической работы.
graphic   work.

A smoother translation of sentence (1)
is:

*The literature (being) included in the
index throws light on the theory and practise
of library and bibliographic work.*

2. Количество периодических изданий
The number of periodic editions

приобретаемых   для международного книгообмена
being acquired for international   exchange

будет   увеличено.
will be increased.

In sentence (2) the present passive
participle приобретаемых is in the genitive
plural case in agreement with the noun it
describes - изданий.

To determine the infinitives for the
participles shown in sentences (1) and (2),
the following procedure is used:

Present Passive Participles:	включаемая
	приобретаемых
Drop case ending:	включаем
	приобретаем

Drop third person plural ending remaining	включ приобрет
Add infinitive ending	включать приобретать

*An Exercise in Translating Adjectives Being
   Compared and Present Passive Participles*

The following sentences are to be translated completely. Translations and explanations are provided on pages 168-171.

1. Конец книги более интересен чем начало.

2. Библиотека имени В. И. Ленина является

найболее крупным в стране центром между-

библиотечного абонемента.

3. Особый интерес представляют библио-

графические обзоры литературы, публикуемые

специалистами в научных журналах.

4. В конце монографии помещены предметный

указатель фамалий цитируемых авторов.

5. Отдел рукописей государственной

библиотеки СССР имени В. И. Ленина - одно из

крупнейших архивохранилищ страны.

TRANSLATION OF EXERCISE ON PAGES 166-167

1. Конец[1]   книги   более   интересен[2]
   The end of the book is more interesting

чем   начало[3]
than the beginning.

2. Библиотека   имени   В. И. Ленина
   The library named for V. I. Lenin

является[4]наиболее крупным[5] в   стране
   is   the largest   in the country

центром междубиблиотечного абонемента.
center   of interlibrary   loan.

   **The following revision of sentence (2)
renders it more readable.**

   *The library named for V. I. Lenin is the
largest center of interlibrary loan in the
country.*

---

[1] кон|ец ...1. end...

[2] An example of the compound comparative used
   predicatively.

[3] начал|о...1. beginning

[4] явля|ться *imperf* -юсь, -ешься,...2. be,
   turn out to be;....

[5] This example of the compound superlative
   degree of an adjective and the noun it
   describes центром, is subject to the instrumental case because of the verb
   являться. Note that the adjective is separ-
   ated from its noun by the phrase в стране.

3. Особый[1]   интерес представляют[2]
   Special interest   present

библиографические обзоры[3] литературы
bibliographic   reviews of literature

публикуемые[4] специалистами   в   научных
being published by specialists in scientific

журналах.
journals.

   **The following revision of sentence (3)
renders it more readable.**

   *Bibliographic reviews of literature
being published by specialists in scientific
journals, present special interest.*

4. В   конце[5]   монографии   помещены[6]
   At the end of the monograph are located

---

[1] особ|ый *a* special....

[2] представл|ять *imperf* -яю,-яешь..1..present

[3] обзор *(m)* N review

[4] This present passive participle is derived
from the familiar verb публиковать. It is
in the nominative plural case modifying the
subject of the sentence обзоры.

[5] кон|ец *m* -ца, -цов 1. end....
This is an example of one of several nouns
which when declined eliminate the vowel in
the stem.

[6] помещ|ать *imperf* ...1. place, put, locate..
This is a shortened form of the past passive participle.

(continued from page 169)

предметный   указатель   и   указатель
the subject   index   and the index

    фамилий[1]   цитируемых[2]   авторов.
of surnames of being quoted authors.

**The following revision of sentence (4)
renders it more readable:**

    *The subject index and the index of sur-
names of authors being quoted, are located
at the end of the monograph.*

    5.   Отдел   рукописей[3]
      The division of manuscripts

государственной библиотеки   СССР
  of the State   Library   of the U.S.S.R.

---

[1] фамили|я *f* -и, -й (sur)name, family name

[2] цитир|овать *imperf*-ую, -уешь, quote, cite
An example of the present passive participle
in the plural genitive case in agreement
with the noun it describes, авторов.

[3] рукопись *(m)* N manuscript

имени   В. И. Ленина -[1]одно[2]из
named for V. I. Lenin is one   of

крупнейших[3]   архивохранилищ[4]
the most important archive depositories

страны.
of the country.

---

[1] When a - is shown in the context of a
sentence, it may be translated as the
present tense of the verb - to be.

[2] оди|о *n ...see* один.
один *I num card & pron indef*..одно *n*,..
1. one...

[3] крупн|ый *a* ...1. large,......2..important.
An example of the simple superlative degree
of an adjective in the plural genitive case
describing the noun which follows. Both
the adjective and noun are subject to the
preposition из which precedes.

[4] The first part of this word is transliterated as *archive*. The second part is:
хранилище *(n)* N storage, depository.
The letter o connects the two words.

Vocabulary

отде́л абонеме́нта	*(m)*	N circulation department
отде́л зака́зов	*(m)*	N order department
обзо́р	*(m)*	N review
обме́н	*(m)*	N exchange
руково́дство	*(n)*	N handbook, manual
ру́копись	*(m)*	N manuscript
храни́лище	*(n)*	N storage, depository

EXERCISE

Translate the following with the use of the dictionary:

1. На выставках была представлена новейшая зарубежная литература.

2. В центральной картотеке будут сосредоточены сведения по предлагаемым и запрашиваемым периодическим изданиям.

3. Важной формой пропаганды литературы являются обзоры наиболее интересных тематических выставок.

4. Теоретические вопросы будут обсуждаться на организуемой библиотекой имени В. И. Ленина всесоюзной теоретический конференции по рекомендательной библиографии.

CHAPTER 12

The Past Active Participle

Three participles commonly found in library literature, the past passive, the present active and the present passive, have been discussed in previous chapters.* There is one other participle - the past active, which should be mastered. It is derived from the masculine past tense of an imperfective or perfective verb and like other participles, performs the function of an adjective in a sentence.

Past Active Participle	Derived from
читавший	читал
прочитавший	прочитал
издававший	издавал
издавший	издал

As shown above, the letters вш (or ш in some irregular cases not shown) with appropriate adjective endings depending on the noun being modified, have replaced the final л of the masculine past tense.

Here are some examples of the past active participle translated in the context of a sentence:

---

*Past passive - Chapter 8, present active - Chapter 10, present passive - Chapter 11.

1. Указатель будет давать название
   The Index will   give   the name

   журнала   опубликовавшего   статью.
of the journal which published the article.

2.   Комиссия   собрала материал
   The Commission collected material

   отражавший   практику
which was reflecting the practise

каталогизации.
of cataloging.

To determine the infinitives for the past active participles in sentences (1) and (2) the following procedure is used:

Past Active Participles:	опубликовавшего
	отражавший
Drop case ending:	опубликовавш
	отражавш
Drop participle ending and return to masc. past tense:	опубликовал
	отражал
Drop masc. past tense ending and add infinitive ending:	опубликовать
	отражать

Negatives

In a simple Russian sentence containing a subject, verb and direct object such as

Издатель   читает   газету.
The publisher is reading the newspaper.

the introduction of the negative sense produces this change:

    Издатель   не читает   газеты.
The publisher is not reading the newspaper.

    The case of the direct object (news-
paper) has been changed from accusative to
genitive.

    If another negative word appears in the
sentence

    Издатель   никогда не читает   газеты.
The publisher never not reads the newspaper.

the word не will also be shown, literally
translated as a double negative but actually
translated as

    The publisher never reads the newspaper.

    The word нет* - *no*, is used in opposi-
tion to да - *yes*. But, if нет appears in a
sentence, it may also be translated in this
manner:

    В библиотеке   нет   книги.
In the library is not the book.

    Книги is in the genitive case because
it is governed by the negative нет. Having
first translated the sentence literally, it
is now possible to change the word order to:

    The book is not in the library.

---

*Actually a contraction of не and есть (an
uncommon form of the verb - to be)

Here is another example of the use of нет in a sentence:

В Финляндии   нет   печатных библио-
In Finland are not printed biblio-

графических   пособий,   адресованных
graphic   textbooks,   addressed

детям.
to children.

A smoother translation of the sentence shown above is:

In Finland, there are no printed biblio-graphic textbooks, addressed to children.

The Conditional Mood of Sentences

The verb form in a sentence expressing the conditional mood is made up of two words - the past tense* of the verb, imperfective or perfective, agreeing with its subject in gender and number, and the particle бы.

Sentences considered to be in the con-ditional mood like

Если бы у библиотекаря была   летопись
If by the librarian was the chronicle
or
(If the librarian had the chronicle)

абонент   её   читал бы
the borrower it would read
or
(the borrower would read it)

---

*See Chapter 9

are composed of two parts - one which presents a condition

Если бы у библиотекаря была летопись
If the librarian had the chronicle

and the other which indicates the result of
the condition presented

абонент её читал бы
the borrower would read it

The particle бы is shown in the conditional portion as well as in that portion of
the sentence which gives the result of the
condition. In the latter, it may follow or
precede the past tense of the imperfective or
perfective verb.

Depending on the context of the sentence
a certain degree of flexibility may be exer-
cised in translating the conditional:

Если бы у библиотекаря была летопись
If the librarian had had the chronicle

вчера, абонент её читал бы.
yesterday, the borrower would have read it.

Often, the result portion of a sentence
will appear without the conditional portion:

книгопродавец   хотел бы получать
The bookseller would like to obtain

заказы.
the orders.

An Exercise in Translating the Past Active
    Participle, the Negative and the Conditional

    The following sentences are to be
translated completely. Translations and explanations are provided on pages 182-185.

    1. На Первом национальном форуме

библиотекарей, проходившем в Гаване

были приняты рекомендации о составлении

новых программ для библиотечного отделения

Гаванского университета.

    2. В наших университетских библиотеках нет

музыкальных отделов.

    3. Международный симпозиум по португало-

бразильским исследованиям рекомендовал

начать издание квартального библиографического

бюллетеня, который учитывал бы произведения

печати (книги, статьи, журнальные и газетные

работы, помещенные в сборниках) вводящие

новые материалы в область португало-

бразильских исследований.

TRANSLATION OF EXERCISE ON PAGES 180-181

1. На Первом   национальном форуме
   At the first   national   forum

библиотекарей,   проходившем[1]   в
of librarians,   which was being held in

Гаване, были приняты[2]   рекомендации   о
Havana, were accepted recommendations about

   составлении   новых   программ для
   the compilation of new programs for

библиотечного отделения Гаванского
the library   section   of Havana

университета.
University.

   The following revision of sentence (1)
renders it more readable.

   *At The First National Forum of Librar-
ians being held in Havana, recommendations
were accepted for the compilation of new
programs for the library section of Havana
University.*

---

[1]проход|ить...6. go off, pass *(of a perform-
ance, lesson, etc)*; повсюду проходят
митинги rallies are held everywhere.

[2]приним|ать *imperf*, прин|ять *perf*..3. accept.
This is a form of the past passive participle.

2. В наших[1] университетских библиотеках
   In   our   university   libraries

   нет   музыкальных[2] отделов.
   are not   music   sections.

   The following revision of sentence (2)
renders it more readable.

   *In our university libraries there are
no music sections.*

3.   Международный   симпозиум по португало-
   The International Symposium on Portuguese-

бразильским исследованиям[3] рекомендовал[4]
Brazilian   research   recommended

начать[5]   издание   квартального[6]
to begin the edition of a quarterly

библиографического бюллетеня, который[7]
  bibliographic   bulletin   which

_____

[1]
 наши *pron pl* -х...*see* наш
 наш *I pron poss corresp to* мы...наша *f,*
 наше *n,*   наши *pl* our; ours

[2]
This adjective and the noun it modifies are
both in the genitive case following the
negative нет

[3]
исследование *(n)* N investigation,research

[4]
Past tense of the verb рекоменд|овать

[5]
начать *see* начинать
начин|ать .....begin...

[6]
квартальный Adj. quarterly

[7]
котор|ый *pron* 1. which

(continued from page 183)

учитывал бы[1]   произведения[2]
would take into account   works

печати[3]   (книги, статьи,[4] журнальные
of the press (books, articles,   journal

и газетные работы,[5] помещенные[6] в
and newspaper works,   located   in

сборниках)   вводящие[7] новые материалы
collections)introducing new materials

---

[1]
учитыв|ать ...take into account
Here is an example of the conditional form
of a verb

[2]
произведение *(n)* N work

[3]
печат|ь *f* -и, -ей ...3. press...

[4]
статья *(f)* N article

[5]
работ|а *f* -ы, *pl* -ы...1. work

[6]
помещ|ать ...1. place, put, locate
An example of the past passive participle

[7]
вввод|ить...1. introduce
An example of the present active participle

в   область[1]   португало -бразильских
into the field of Portuguese-Brazilian

исследований.
research.

---

[1]област|ь   *f* ...2. field, province, sphere

Vocabulary

абоне́нт	*(m)*	N	borrower
зака́з	*(m)*	N	order
иссле́дование	*(n)*	N	investigation, research, paper
кварта́льный		Adj.	quarterly
книгопрода́вец	*(m)*	N	bookseller
ле́топись	*(f)*	N	chronicle
отделе́ние	*(n)*	N	part, section
произведе́ние	*(n)*	N	work
статья́	*(f)*	N	article
экземпля́р	*(m)*	N	copy

EXERCISE

Translate the following with the use of the dictionary:

1. Отдел подготовил и издал каталог иностранных карт и атласов, поступивших в библиотеку.

2. Альтернативное правило дано для периодических изданий, изменивших свое заглавие.

3. Почему вы не читаете английской газеты?

4. Создание специального научно-исслед- овательского института, отметил В. И. Шунков, позволало бы поднять на более высокий уровень теоретическую работу в области библиотеко- ведения и библиографии.

CHAPTER 13

The Gerund

The gerund is a verbal adverb which like the participle* (or verbal adjective) is derived from a verb. Unlike the participle, the gerund performs the function of an adverb in a sentence in that it modifies a verb. In addition, the gerund, like other adverbs, does not change according to gender and number and is not declined.

The Present Gerund

The present gerund may be traced to the third person plural of the present tense of an imperfective infinitive:

Present Gerund	Derived from	Infinitive
читая	читают	читать
публикуя	публикуют	публиковать
составляя	составляют	составлять

Examples of the present gerund in the context of a sentence are:

1. Каждый ребёнок, <u>приходя</u> в библиотеку,
   Each child, coming into the library,

заполняет стандартную карточку.
completes a standard card.

---

*Discussed in Chapters 8, 10, 11 and 12.

2.   Отдел   продолжал осуществлять
   The division continued to carry out

централизованную каталогизацию текущих
   centralized   cataloging   of current

карт,   <u>издавая</u>   печатную   карточку.
cards, while publishing the printed   card.

From these examples, it should be noted
that:

1. The present gerund indicates an action
which accompanies another verb in the sentence.

2. The present gerund and the verb it
accompanies have the same subject.

To determine the infinitives for the
present gerunds shown in sentences (1) and
(2), the following procedure is used:

Present Gerunds:	приходя издавая
Replace gerund ending with third person plural ending:	приходят издавают

Replace third person plural
   ending with infinitive
   ending:
	приходить
	издавать

The Past Gerund

The past gerund may be traced to the
masculine past tense of a perfective verb:

Past Gerund	Derived from	Infinitive
прочитав **(or)** прочитавши	прочитал	прочитать

Past Gerund	Derived from	Infinitive
издав **(or)** издавши	издал	издать

Examples of the past gerund in the context of a sentence are:

1. <u>Написав</u>   сочинение он отдал его
    Having written the work he sent it

издателю.
to the publisher.

2. <u>Изучив</u>   русский   язык
    Having studied the Russian language

она начала переводить рецензии рассказов.
she began to translate reviews of stories.

It should be noted that the action of the past gerund is completed before the action of the verb it accompanies.

Auxiliary Words

In Chapter 8 the verb быть was shown as an auxiliary to a verb infinitive to produce the future imperfective tense. Here are some other words which are seen as auxiliaries to verbs. Note that the translation of the verb infinitive and its auxiliary is not a literal one:

1.   Иллюстрации   не <u>могут</u>* дать
      The illustrations not can   give

---

*The irregular present tense of the verb мочь.
мочь *imperf* могу, можешь, могут...be able

полного   представления   о   процессах.
the complete   idea   about the processes.

2.   Конференция должна*решить
     The conference should decide

вопросы   теории рекомендательной
the questions of theory of a recommended

библиографии.
bibliography.

The Old and New Orthography

The alphabet first presented in Chapter
I and used throughout this text is the one
used in Russia since the Revolution in 1917.
Here are some other letters which appear in
words found in literature of the pre-revolution era. They are shown with their present
day equivalents:

Old	Transliteration	New
I i	$\bar{\text{i}}$	и
Ѣ ѣ	$\widehat{\text{ie}}$	е
Ѳ ѳ	$\dot{\text{f}}$	ф
Ѵ ѵ	$\dot{\text{y}}$	и

Here are some **further** notes regarding
changes which have taken place:

---

*долж|ен *predic* -на, ⁻но, ⁻ны 1...must;
   should; ought (to);

1. According to ALA Rules* the new
Russian orthography is to used for headings
of catalog cards for pre-revolution literature.

2. *Titles* of pre-revolution literature
are to be **ex**actly transcribed for catalog
cards, thus transliterating the old letters
as shown above, when necessary.

3. The letter ъ (hard sign) appearing
in pre-revolution literature as the final
letter of many words like

переводъ
сборникъ

is now omitted from that position and appears
now only in the middle of words (see Chapter
I).

4. The pre-revolution genitive and accusative endings of adjectives аго and яго
are today equivalent to ого and его respect-
ively.

*An Exercise in Translating the Gerunds and
   Auxiliary Words*

The following sentences are to be translated completely. Completed translations and
explanations are provided on pages 195-197.

------

*Clara Beetle, Editor, *A. L. A. Cataloging
Rules for Author and Title Entries,* second
edition, American Library Association,
Chicago, 1949.

(continued from page 193)

1. Он должен, широко используя библиографические пособия, осуществлять комплектование массовых библиотеках, учитывая
количество и состав читателей.

2. Дав краткий исторический очерк развития
проблемы централизованного хранения библиотечных фондов, автор переходит к описанию
организации резервных фондов отдельных
крупных библиотек.

3. Подумав ещё немного и учитывая
предыдущий текст, переводчик сделает ещё одно
исправление и перепишет фразу.

TRANSLATION OF EXERCISE ON PAGE 194

1. Он должен,[1] широко[2] используя[3] библио-
   He should, widely   using   biblio-

графические пособия, осуществлять[4]
graphical textbooks, carry out

комплектование   массовых[5]   библиотеках,
the acquisition of the public libraries,

       учитывая[6]   количество[7]
taking into account the number

---

[1] долж|ен *predic* -на, -но, -ны 1...must;
should; ought (to);

[2] The adverbial form of the adjective
широкий - wide

[3] The present gerund of the verb
использ|овать *perf & imperf*...use, utilize..

[4] осуществл|ять *imperf*...carry out, realize..
The auxiliary for this verb infinitive is
должен (see [1])

[5] массовая библиотека *(f)* Adj.N public library

[6] The present gerund of the verb
учитыв|ать *imperf*... take into account

[7] количеств|о *n* -а quantity, amount;number

(continued from page 195)

и   состав[1]   читателей
and composition of the readers.

  2.   Дав[2]   краткий   исторический
      Having given a short   historical

очерк[3]   развития[4]   проблемы
sketch of the development of the problem

централизованного хранения   библиотечных
  of centralized   storage   of library

фондов,   автор   переходит[5] к   описанию[6]
stocks, the author   turns   to a description

   организации   резервных   фондов
of the organization of reserve   stocks

---

[1]состав *m*...1. composition

[2]Past gerund of the verb-дать *see* давать
дав|ать *imperf*...1. give...

[3]очерк *(m)* N essay, sketch

[4]развити|е *n* -я development

[5]переход|ить *imperf* перехожу,переходишь..turn

[6]Although in library terminology this is de-
fined as *entry*, the dictionary definition
описани|е *n* -я, -й description...
seems to fit better in this case.

отдельных[1] крупных[2] библиотек.
of separate large libraries.

3.   Подумав[3]   ещё[4] немного[5]   и
       Having thought still somewhat and

       учитывая[6]   предыдущий[7] текст
taking into account the previous text,

       переводчик[8]   сделает[9]   ещё[10]   одно
the translator will make still one (one more)

---

[1] отдельн|ый *a* separate

[2] крупный *Adj.* big, large

[3] Past gerund of the verb
подум|ать *perf.*. 1.*see* думать
дум|ать *imperf,* подумать *perf* 1. think...

[4] ещё *adv* ..3. still...

[5] немного *adv*... 2. somewhat...

[6] Present gerund of the verb
учитыв|ать *imperf* ..take into account

[7] предыдущ|ий *a* ..previous

[8] переводчик *m* ..translator

[9] сделать *see* делать
дел|ать *imperf* -аю,-аешь, с|делать *perf*.make

[10] See [4]

(continued from page 197)

исправление[1]   и   перепишет[2]   фразу.
correction   and will rewrite the phrase.

---

[1]The exact form of this noun does not appear
in the dictionary. The definition given for
the verb infinitive related to the noun is
исправл|ять...2. correct

[2]Since this appears to be an irregularly conjugated verb, in order to determine the
infinitive, let us first divide the word
into prefix пере and suffix пишет. The
dictionary lists the suffix conjugated as
пишу, пишешь..*see* писать
We now know that the verb infinitive is
переписать *see* переписывать
переписыв|ать *imperf*..перепи|сать..rewrite

Vocabulary

кру́пный		Adj.	big, large
ма́ссовая библиоте́ка	*(f)*	Adj. N	public library
о́черк	*(m)*	N	sketch, essay
расска́з	*(m)*	N	story
реце́нзия	*(f)*	N	review
сочине́ние	*(n)*	N	work

EXERCISE

*Translate the following with the use of the
dictionary:*

1. Работая с дошкольниками, библиотекари
могли бы оказать большую помощь учителям
в расширении кругозора детей.

2. Примером может служить библиотека
британского музея в Лондоне.

3. Изучив русский язык, я начала переводить
романы.

4. Рассказав директору о случае на библиотеке
библиотекарь засмеялся.

CHAPTER 14

Numerals

The subject of numerals will be discussed in two parts - cardinal numerals which
denote the number of objects, and ordinal
numerals which denote their order.

Cardinal Numerals

Cardinal numerals do not always agree
with the adjectives and nouns that follow
them. In addition, the rules governing the
cases of these adjectives and nouns defy
logical explanation. Suffice it to say that
the reader should be cognizant of the fact
that the usual rules of grammar cannot be
applied to numerals. Here are several examples which bear this out:

Она читает одну газету ежедневно.
She reads one newspaper every day.

Она читает   сто   одну страницу ежедневно.
She reads one hundred one pages every day.

The noun following один, одна, одно
(one) and compound numbers ending with *one*
will be in the singular and in the same case
as the numeral.

Она читает три   газеты   ежедневно.
She reads three newspapers every day.

The noun following два *(two)*, три
(three) or четыре *(four)* which is in the

201

nominative or accusative case, will be in the genitive singular.

Она читает три хороших газеты ежедневно.
She reads three good newspapers every day.

Adjectives though, following these numerals will be in the genitive plural.

Она читает шесть хороших газет   ежедневно.
She   reads   six   good newspapers   every day.

Adjectives and nouns following all other numerals in the nominative or accusative cases will be in the genitive plural.

Она   читает   вестник   трём
She is reading the review to three

советским писателям.
Soviet   writers.

Издатель   перепечатал   словарь
The publisher   reprinted the dictionary

со ста восемью новыми страницами.
with 100   eight   new   pages.

Any other numeral (except один and compounds) used in cases other than the nominative and accusative requires both noun and accompanying adjective in the plural and in the same case as the numeral.

In their declension, cardinal numerals take on characteristics of both nouns and adjectives. Irregularities should be noted:

один *(one)*

Case	Masculine	Feminine	Neuter
N	один	одна	одно
G	одного	одной	одного
D	одному	одной	одному
A	один	одну	одно
I	одним	одной	одним
P	одном	одной	одном

	два*(two)	три*(three)	четыре* (four)
N	два, две	три	четыре
G	двух	трёх	четырёх
D	двум	трём	чотырём
A	два, две	три	четыре
I	двумя	тремя	четырьмя
P	двух	трёх	четырёх

   Numerals ending with the letter ь are declined like feminine nouns ending with the same letter:

	пять*(five)	восемь* (eight)	двадцать* (twenty)
N	пять	восемь	двадцать
G	пяти	восьми	двадцати
D	пяти	восьми	двадцати
A	пять	восемь	двадцать
I	пятью	восемью	двадцатью
P	пяти	восьми	двадцати

   Some numerals like пятьдесят *(fifty)* and пятьсот *(five hundred)* are composed of two parts both of which are declined:

---

*The numeral два (two) is used in the nominative case with masculine and neuter nouns. две is used with feminine nouns. The other numerals have one form for all genders.

Case	пятьдесят (fifty)	пятьсот* (five hundred)
N	пятьдесят	пятьсот
G	пятидесяти	пятисот
D	пятидесяти	пятистам
A	пятьдесят	пятьсот
I	пятьюдесятью	пятьюстами
P	пятидесяти	пятистах

Ordinal Numerals

Ordinal numerals beyond *two* are similar to cardinal numerals:

Cardinal		Ordinal	
один	*one*	первый	*first*
два	*two*	второй	*second*
три	*three*	третий	*third*
четыре	*four*	четвёртый	*fourth*
пять	*five*	пятый	*fifth*
восемь	*eight*	восьмой	*eighth*
двадцать	*twenty*	двадцатый	*twentieth*
пятьдесят	*fifty*	пятидесятый	*fiftieth*
сто	*100*	сотый	*hundredth*
пятьсот	*500*	пятьсотый	*five hundredth*

They are unlike cardinal numerals in that all are declined like adjectives and agree in number, gender and case with the nouns following. For example:

Она читает первый оттиск.
She is reading the first reprint.

---

*The irregular declension of one hundred (сто in the nominative and accusative, ста in all other cases) becomes even more irregular in compound numerals.

In sentences with compound ordinal numerals like:

Он   читает   вестник   о
He is reading the review about

    сто   пятьдесят восьмой сказке.
the one hundred fifty eighth story.

it should be noted that only the final numeral is ordinal and agrees with the noun following - the other numerals are cardinal in the nominative case.

Ordinal numerals are also shown in an abbreviated form such as:

В   1-ой   главе   список
In the first chapter (there is) a list

путеводителей.
of guidebooks.

In this example, 1-ой is an abbreviation for первой in the prepositional case.

Words to be Wary of

Besides the fact that odd groupings of words are sometimes idioms, the translator should be aware that there are a number of small words in the Russian language used in special ways which may also be confusing. Here are a few - the dictionary should be consulted in cases where the translation of other words seem questionable:

1.   Второе   издание   книги,
1. The second edition of the book,

так же как и   первое   плохо
just as   the first, is poorly

иллюстрировано.
illustrated.

2. Как общие   так и отраслевые
2. *Both general and   branch*

библиографические указатели   даны.
bibliographic   indexes   are given.

3. Причина   этого   не   только в
3. *The cause of this is not only   in*

недостаточных   тиражах   отдельных
the inadequate printings of individual

пособий   но   и в   том   что
textbooks, but also in the fact that

введение   плохо   организовано.
the introduction is poorly   organized.

Adjectives used as Nouns

Another point of confusion may occur
when certain adjectives stand alone with no
nouns to modify. They are idiomatically
used as nouns and are perfectly legal. Some
of them are:

данные   *data*

рабочий *worker*

учёный   *scientist, scholar*

The Republics of Russia

    The librarian will come across publica-
tions from other republics of the Soviet
Union and should be aware that there are 15
such republics:

Азербайджанская ССР*	*Azerbaidzhan Soviet Socialist Republic*
Армянская	*Armenian*
Белорусская	*Belorussian*
Грузинская	*Georgian*
Казахская	*Kazakh*
Киргизская	*Kirghiz*
Латвийская	*Latvian*
Литовская	*Lithuanian*
Молдавская	*Moldavian*
Таджикская	*Tadjik*
Туркменская	*Turkmen*
Узбекская	*Uzbek*
Украйнская	*Ukrainian*
Эстонская	*Estonian*
РСФСР - Российская Советская Федеративная Социалистическая Республика	*Russian Soviet Federative Socialist Republic*

    Here are some of the republics in
abbreviated form:

Азерб.ССР	*Azerbaidzhan SSR*
БССР	*Belorussian SSR*
Груз.ССР	*Georgian SSR*
Турк.ССР	*Turkmen SSR*
Узб.ССР	*Uzbek SSR*
Эстон.ССР	*Estonian SSR*

---

*See Chapter 4, page 71.

An Exercise in Translating Numerals

The following sentences are to be translated completely. Translations and explanations are provided on pages 209-210.

1. Издатель работал с четырьмя старыми

библиотекарями и ста восемью молодыми

студентами на двадцати трёх новых библиотеках.

2. Библиотекари купили двадцать четыре

дорогих русских книги. Одна из них стоит

триста пятьдесят рублей. Другая книга ещё

дороже первой и стоит пятьсот двадцать пять

рублей.

3. Франция является третьим государством

ратифицировавшим вторую из этих конвенций.

Конвенция ратифицирована двумя другими

государствами: Цейлоном и Израйлем.

1.   Издатель   работал   с четырьмя
     The publisher worked   with   four

старыми библиотекарями и   ста
  old   librarians   and one hundred

восемью молодыми студентами на двадцати
 eight   young   students   in   twenty

трёх новых библиотеках.
three   new   libraries.

2. Библиотекари   купили[1]двадцать четыре
   The librarians bought   twenty   four

дорогих[2] русских[2]книги[3] Одна[4]из них   стоит[5]
expensive Russian books.   One   of them costs

---

[1]купить *see* покупать
покуп|ать *imperf..,*куп|ить *perf* -лю,купишь,
....buy.

[2]дорог|ой   -ая,-ое,-ие,...expensive
This adjective is in the genitive plural
since it follows the numeral четыре in the
accusative case.

[3]This noun following the numeral четыре is
in the genitive singular case.

[4]This feminine numeral refers to the noun
книга in the preceding sentence.

[5]сто|ить *imperf* -ю, -ищь, ..cost

(continued from page 209)

триста   пятьдесят рублей. Другая[1]
three hundred   fifty   rubles. Another

книга   ещё   дороже[2]   первой[3]
book is even more expensive than the first

 и стоит   пятьсот   двадцать пять рублей.
and costs five hundred   twenty   five rubles.

3. Франция является третьим[4] государством[4]
    France   is   the third   state

ратифицировавшим   вторую   из этих[5]
   ratifying   the second of these

 конвенций.   Конвенция ратифицирована
conventions. The convention is ratified

двумя другими государствами: Цейлоном и
by two other   states: Ceylon and

Израйлем.
  Israel.

---

[1]друг|ой *I a* -ая,-ое,-ие other..another...

[2]This is the simple comparative form of the adjective дорогой. (see Chapter 11).

[3]первый *(first)* is in the genitive singular case following a comparative adjective.

[4]Adjective and noun are in the instrumental case required by являться preceding.

[5]этих *gen, acc & pr* of эти; *see* этот
этот *I pron dem*...эти *pl* this

Vocabulary

оттиск	(m)	N	reprint
перепеча́тывать перепеча́тать	Imperf. verb Perf. verb		to reprint
путеводи́тель	(m)	N	guidebook
ска́зка	(f)	N	story, tale
слова́рь	(m)	N	dictionary
спи́сок	(m)	N	list
тира́ж	(m)	N	edition, printing

EXERCISE

*Translate the following with the use of the
dictionary:*

1. В библиотеке шесть тысяч пятьсот шесть-
десят книг.

2. Центральная библиотека пользуется меж-
библиотечным абонементом с пятьюдесятью
библиотеками Советского союза и зарубежных
государств.

3. Книжная палата оказывает большую помощь
двадцати пяти массовым библиотикам республики,
выпуская для них печатные карточки
централизованной каталогизации.

RUSSIAN-ENGLISH ALPHABETICAL LISTING
OF LIBRARY TERMS

Abbreviations used:

m	masculine
f	feminine
n	neuter
N	noun
Adj.	adjective
pl.	plural
V	verb (imperfective and perfective)

а

абонемент *m* N subscription, loan
абонент *m* N borrower
адресная книга *f* Adj. N directory
академия наук *f* N N Academy of Sciences
альманах *m* N almanac
анналы pl. annals
антикварный Adj. secondhand

б

библиографический Adj. bibliographic
библиография *f* N bibliography
библиотека отделения *f* N, *n* N department
     library
библиотечный Adj. library
библиотекарь *m* N librarian
библиотечное дело *n* Adj. N library science
библиотековедение *n* N library science
библиотечный институт *m* Adj. N library school
бюллетень *m* N bulletin
брошюра *f* N pamphlet

бумага *f* N paper

в

в печати Idiom in press
введение *n* N preface, introduction
век *m* N century
вестник *m* N review
всесоюзный Adj. all-union, national, federal
второй Adj. second
выдержка *f* N excerpt
выпуск *m* issue, number, part, edition
выходной лист *m* Adj. N title-page

г

газета *f* N newspaper
глава *f* N chapter
год *m* N year
годовой Adj. annual
государственный Adj. state, national
грубая классификация *f* Adj. N broad class-
    ification

д

дата издания *f* N, *n* N date of publication
десятичная классификиция *f* Adj. N decimal
    classification
директор библиотеки *m* N, *f* N head librarian
дисконт *m* N discount
добавочное описание *n* Adj. N added entry
добавлять, добавить V to add
доклад *m* N report
дополнение *n* N addition
дублет *m* N duplicate
двухлетний Adj. biennial
двухмесячный Adj. bimonthly

е

ежегодник *m* N annual, yearbook
ежегодный Adj. yearly
ежедневный Adj. daily
ежеквартальник *m* N quarterly
ежемесячный Adj. monthly
еженедельный Adj. weekly

ж

журнал *m* N journal

з

заглавие *n* N title
заглавный лист *m* Adj. N title page
заказ *m* N order
зарубежный Adj. foreign
знак *m* N mark, sign
знак тома *m* N N volume number

и

и другие Idiom and others
и так далее Idiom etcetera
избранные произведения pl. selected
     works
известие *n* N news, information
извлечение *n* N extract
издание *n* N edition
издатель *m* N publisher
издательство *n* publishing house
издавать, издать V to publish
изменять, изменить V to revise
иллюстрированный Adj. illustrated
имени Idiom named for
именной указатель *m* Adj. N author index
иностранный Adj. foreign
использованная литература *f* Adj. N sources
исправлять, исправить V to revise
исследование *n* N contribution, paper, research

исчерпывать, исчерпать V to exhaust

К

карманный словарь *m* Adj. N pocket dictionary
картина *f* N picture, illustration
картотека *f* N card file
карточка *f* N card
карточный шкаф *m* Adj. N catalog case
квартал *m* N quarter
квартальный Adj. quarterly
кварто *m* N quarto
классификатор *m* N classifier
книга *f* N book
книгоиздатель *m* N publisher
книгоиздательство *n* N publishing house
книгообмен *m* N exchange
книгопродавец *m* N bookseller
книготорговец *m* N bookseller
книготорговля *f* N booktrade
книжный фонд *m* Adj. N bookstock,
      holdings
книжная лавка *f* N bookstore
книжный магазин *m* N bookstore
коллективный автор *m* Adj. N corporate author
комплектование *n* N acquisition
конспект *m* N compendium, synopsis
копейка *f* N kopeck
краска *f* N color
краткий Adj. short
краткое изложение *n* Adj. N summary
крупный Adj. big, large
курсив *m* N italics

Л

летопись *f* N chronicle
лист *m* N leaf, sheet
литература *f* N literature

M

малый Adj. small
магазин *m* N store
массовая библиотека *f* Adj. N public library
месячный Adj. monthly
месяц *m* N month
междубиблиотечный interlibrary
международный Adj. international
Москва *f* N Moscow

Н

название *n* N title
народный Adj. national
наука *f* N science
научная библиотека *f* Adj. N research library
научный Adj. scientific, scholarly
новый Adj. new
номер *m* N number

О

обмен *m* N exchange
обозрение *n* N review
обрабатывать, обработать V to edit
обслуживание *n* N service
общество *n* N society, association
оглавление *n* N table of contents
опечатка *f* N typographical error
описание *n* N entry
описание под заглавием Idiom title entry
основная карточка *f* Adj. N main card
основное описание *n* Adj. N main entry
отдел *m* N division, section
отдел абонемента *m* N N circulation department
отдел заказов *m* N N order department
отделение *n* N part, section
отпечатывать, отпечатать V to print
отраслевая библиотека *f* Adj. N special library
оттиск *m* N reprint
отсчёт *m* N report, account

отсылка *f* N reference
очерк *m* N essay, sketch

п

первый Adj. first
перевод *m* N translation
переделка *f* N adaptation
перепечатывать, перепечатать V to reprint
перепечатка *f* N reprint
переплетать, переплести V to bind
переплёт *m* N binding
переплётчик *m* binder
пересматривать, пересмотреть V to revise
периодический Adj. periodical, serial
печатать, напечатать V to print
печатный Adj. printed
писатель *m* N author
письмо *n* N letter
под редакцией Idiom edited by
подзаголовок *m* N subtitle, subheading
подписка *f* N subscription
поиски информации *m* N, *f* N information re-
полное издание *n* Adj. N complete |trieval
полный Adj. complete |edition
половина *f* N half
полугодовный Adj. half yearly
полутом *m* N half volume
пособие *n* N textbook
предисловие *n* N preface, introduction
предметный Adj. subject
прибавление *n* N appendix, supplement
продолжение *n* N continuation
произведение *n* N work
просматривать, просмотреть V to revise
псевдоним *m* N pseudonym
публиковать, опубликовать V to publish
публичная библиотека *f* Adj. N public library
путеводитель *m* N guidebook

р

рассказ *m* N story
редактировать, отредактировать V to edit
редактор *m* N editor
редкий Adj. rare
реферат *m* N abstract
реферативный журнал *m* Adj. N abstract
                                        journal
рецензия *f* N review
рубль *m* N ruble
рубрика *f* N heading
руководство *n* N handbook, manual
рукопись *m* N manuscript

с

сборник *m* N collection
сводный каталог *m* Adj. N union catalog
систематический каталог *m* Adj. N classified
                                        catalog
сказка *f* N story, tale, fairy tale
словарь *m* N dictionary
снимок *m* N photograph
соавтор *m* N joint author, co-author
собрание *n* N collection
собрание сочинений Idiom collected works
Совет *m* N Soviet
содержание *n* N table of contents
сокращать, сократить V to shorten, abridge
сообщения *f* N proceedings
составитель *m* N compiler
составление *n* N compilation
сотрудник *m* N co-worker
сочинение *n* N work
список *m* N list
справочная библиотека *f* Adj. N reference
                                        library
справочник *m* N reference book
ссылка *f* N reference
статья *f* N article
страница *f* N page
схема *f* N diagram, chart

Т

таблица *f* N table, plate
тираж *m* N edition, printing
титул *m* N title
то есть Idiom that is
том *m* N volume
трёхмесячный Adj. quarterly
труды pl. works

У

увеличивать, увеличить V to enlarge
указатель *m* N index
умножать, умножить V to enlarge
Универсальная Десятичная
      Классификация *f* Adj. Adj. N Universal
                          Decimal Classification
учебник *m* N textbook

ф

фонд *m* N stock, holding
формат *m* N size, format

х

хороший Adj. good
хранение *n* N storage
хранилище *n* N bookstacks
хроника *f* N chronicle
художественная литература *f* Adj. N fiction,
                         belles-lettres

ц

цена *f* N price
цифра *f* N figure

ч

часть *f* N part

число *n* N date, number
читальный зал *m* Adj. N reading room
читатель *m* N reader

ш

широкий Adj. wide, broad
шмуцтитул *m* N half-title
шрифт *m* N print, type

э

экземпляр *m* N copy

я

язык *m* N language

RUSSIAN-ENGLISH ALPHABETICAL LISTING
OF ABBREVIATIONS*

АН СССР (Академия Наук СССР)USSR Academy of
                                      Sciences
б-фия (библиография)bibliography
б.г. (без года)no date
б-ка (библиотека)library
д. (доллар)dollar
В. (Восток)East
в. (век)century
ВКП (Всесоюзная Коммунистическая Партия)
                    All-Union Communist Party
вв. (века)centuries
вып. (выпуск) issue, edition
г. (год, город) year, city
гг. (годы, города) years, cities
д. (доллар) dollar
ж. (журнал) periodical
З. (Запад) West
ин-т (институт) institute
и.т.д. (и так далее) etcetera
к-т, ком-т (комитет) committee
кн. (книга) book
ком. (комиссия) commission
Л., Лнг., Лнгр. (Ленинград) Leningrad
л. (лист) leaf
лит., лит-ра (литература) literature
лл. (листы) leaves
М. (Москва) Moscow
н., нар. (народный) national
науч., научн. (научный) scientific,scholarly

---

*Library terms from which abbreviations are
 derived are shown in parenthesis.

нац. (национальный) national
о-во (общество) society, association
обозр. (обозрение) review
огл. (оглавление) table of contents
ориг. (оригинальный) original
отд., отдел. (отделение) division, section
отт. (оттиск) reprint
офиц. (официальный) official
пер. (переплёт, перевод) binding, translation
приб.(прибавление) appendix, supplement
прод. (продолжение) continuation
псевд. (псевдоним) pseudonym
р., руб. (рубль) ruble
разд. (раздел) division, section
ред. (редактор) editor
русск. (русский) Russian
с. (сантиметр, серия, страница) centimeter,
                                        series, page
сб. (сборник) collection
сер. (серия) series
см. (сантиметр) centimeter
см. (смотри) see
собр. (собрание) collection
сов. (совет, советский) Soviet
сокр. (сокращение) abbreviation, abridgement
сост. (составитель) compiler
СССР (Союз Советских Социалистических
                                    Республик)
        Union of Soviet Socialist Republics
                                        (USSR)
стр. (страница) page
США (Соединённые Штаты Америки) United States
                        of America (USA)
т. (том, тысяча) volume, thousand
таб. (таблица) table, chart
т. е. (то есть) that is, i. e.
тех., техн. (технический) technical
тит. (титул) title
тит. л. (титульный лист) title page
ук. (указатель) index
ун-т (университет) university
учеб. (учебник) textbook

факс. (факсимиле) facsimile
фиг. (фигура) figure
форм. (формат) size, format
фот. (фотография) photograph
хор. (хороший) good
худож. (художественный) artistic
ц. (цена) price
ч. (часть, число) part, number
чч. (части) parts
экз. (экземпляр) copy